Federalism In Peril

Federalism In Peril

National Unity, Individualism, Free Markets, and the Emerging Global Economy

Edited by
A.R. Riggs and Tom Velk
North American Studies
McGill University

The Fraser Institute
Vancouver, British Columbia, Canada

Canadian Cataloguing in Publication Data

Main entry under title:

Federalism in peril

Includes bibliographical references.
ISBN 0-88975-141-2

1. Federal government—Canada. 2. Canada—
Constitutional law—Amendments. 3. Federal-
provincial relations—Canada.* I. Velk, Tom,
1938-   II. Riggs, A.R. (Alvin Richard),
1931-   III. Fraser Institute (Vancouver, B.C.)
JL27.F43 1992   342.71'03   C92-091125-0

Contents

Section V: Making Federalism Work

Preface

IN 1978 THE FRASER INSTITUTE published a book called *Canadian Confedera-tion at the Crossroads* which explored how constitutional reform might produce a more workable balance of powers between the federal and provincial governments. The conclusion was that we should aim to decentralize the Canadian confederation as both a desirable economic stratagem and as a means of making Canada more flexible in responding to changes in attitudes regarding the respective roles of the federal and provincial governments. The reformed and repatriated constitution did not reflect these conclusions.

Perhaps because the reformed constitution did not reflect the underlying pressures for change, not much has changed since 1978. Once again Canada is at a crossroads, perhaps one from which parts of Canada will choose divergent pathways because they have found the trade-offs that have increasingly been required in the context of the federal structure too difficult or too costly to make. This book concerns itself with various aspects of Canada's federal structure and how it may be transformed in the face of this latest challenge. It is more a book of explorations than of particular solutions but then none of the solutions which have been offered seem likely to be effective.

The Fraser Institute has been pleased to co-operate with the Center for North American Studies at McGill University in publishing this volume. However, the authors of the various contributions have worked independently and their views may not conform to those of the Members or Board of Trustees of the Fraser Institute. We are pleased to offer this book as another contribution to the debate about Canada's future in the hope that it may provoke constructive thinking along productive lines.

Michael A. Walker

Acknowledgements

WE THANK MOST PARTICULARLY Mrs. George Packer Berry of Princeton, New Jersey, whose generous gift, the Gerald Wilkinson endowment, allows McGill's North American Studies (NAS) Program to sponsor conferences on academic matters and issues of public policy. This is the third volume in a series of occasional NAS publications, all completed with the help of the endowment.

We also thank McGill's Department of Economics for financial support and the staff of Ontario's Interchange consortium for their helpful advice. Organization and support were provided by John Farrugia (Interchange—Mohawk College), John McCallum and Pat Tuck (McGill). Michael Walker of the Fraser Institute brought the publishing wing of the Fraser Institute into service, and Bill Watson furnished us with an accurate transcript of the Trudeau breakfast seminar. All the typists in McGill's departments of Economics and Political Science, in particular Michele Lee and Ronda Hazam, at one time or another helped prepare the text.

Our thanks to all of those people, without whom this book could not have been produced. Any errors and omissions are, of course, the fault of the editors.

About the Contributors

D.A.L. Auld is the president of Loyalist College, Belleville, Ontario.

Andrew Cohen is a senior editor and columnist for the *Financial Post*, Toronto.

Thomas J. Courchene is Jarislowsky-Deutsch Professor of Economics and Director of the School of Policy Studies at Queen's University, Kingston, Ontario.

Andrew Coyne, a former columnist for the *Financial Post*, currently writes for the *Globe and Mail*, Toronto.

Charles F. Doran is Andrew Mellon Professor of International Relations at the Paul Nitze School of Advanced International Studies, Johns Hopkins University, Washington, D.C.

David Frum is assistant features editor for the *Wall Street Journal*, New York.

Earl H. Fry is Endowed Professor of Canadian Studies and Political Science, Brigham Young University, Provo, Utah.

Jagdish Handa is Professor of Economics and Associate Dean of the Faculty of Arts, McGill University, Montreal.

William Johnson is a featured columnist for *The Gazette*, Montreal.

Verna Lawrence, an American Indian, is an elected city official, Sault Ste. Marie, Michigan.

Eric Maldoff, a practising Montreal attorney, is a former president of the anglophone rights group, Alliance Quebec.

R.S. McCall is Professor of Philosophy, McGill University.

John McCallum, Dean (Elect) of Arts and Sciences, is Professor and Chairman, Department of Economics, McGill University.

André Raynauld, a former president of the Canadian Economics Association, is Professor of Economics at the Université de Montréal.

A.R. Riggs is Associate Professor of History and Director of North American Studies, McGill University.

Stephen A. Scott, a practising attorney, is a Professor in the Faculty of Law, McGill University.

The Right Honourable Pierre Elliott Trudeau, Former Prime Minister of Canada, lives in Montreal.

Tom Velk, Associate Professor of Economics at McGill University, is also a freelance television journalist.

Michael A. Walker is Executive Director of The Fraser Institute, Vancouver, British Columbia.

William G. Watson, Associate Professor of Economics, McGill University, is a columnist for the *Financial Post* of Toronto and Visiting Professor (1991-92) at Simon Fraser University.

Robert A. Young, of the University of Western Ontario's Political Science department is currently a Visiting Research Fellow at the Institute of Intergovernmental Relations and the School of Policy Studies, Queen's University, Kingston.

Introduction

A.R. Riggs and Tom Velk

IT HAS BEEN TEN YEARS since Prime Minister Pierre Elliott Trudeau initiated the process of patriating the Canadian constitution with a charter of rights, a process which required approval by the British Parliament at Westminster and the provinces of Canada. By his own admission, the Prime Minister "took what he could get"—a flawed document (flawed with the help of the Supreme Court of Canada) which failed to lodge sovereignty in the people, left for future consideration the division of powers and included a notwithstanding clause that allowed the federal or provincial governments to suspend Charter rights through a vote of representative assemblies.

The Charter of Rights and Freedoms gained the approval of all provincial premiers except Quebec's René Lévesque who, intent on preserving the province's French Language, culture and legal system, insisted on additional guarantees that could be translated into a special status within the federation. At the close of the 1980s, the Meech Lake Accord, engineered by provincial premiers meeting in closed session, included a "distinct society" concession for Quebec. It failed, however, to satisfy a strain of rising nationalism in the French province, and it distressed many western Canadians who interpreted the clause as one that Quebec might use to gain special privileges. The West's fears were partially confirmed when Quebec, invoking the notwithstanding clause, refused to comply with a Supreme Court ruling that its language laws offended civil liberties.

The discredited Meech Lake Accord has since been superseded (September 1991) by a new plan to keep Canada united, itself a reaction to the National Assembly of Quebec's startling Bill 150, which promised a provincial referendum on independence by October 1992. The new "discussion document" issued by the federal government makes a lunge in the direction of decentralization. Ottawa would recognize a "distinct society," grant the provinces authority over job training, mining, forestry, tourism, recreation and housing, and increase their authority over the Bank of Canada, immigration and cultural matters; in return, Ottawa's predominance over the economy would be recognized, chiefly in the area of provincial trade barriers that hamper economic development. Although introduced by the Mulroney government with a promise of full and complete consultation with the people of Canada, the plan has been warily received by a public vexed and exhausted by a decade of unrealized expectations.

What indeed should a Canadian constitution contain, and how should it be implemented? These questions were addressed at Montreal's McGill University in May 1991, with the participation of former prime minister Pierre Trudeau and two dozen North American scholars, lawyers, journalists and other experts on public policy issues. The two-day symposium, sponsored by McGill's North American Studies Program—with aid from the Economics department and Interchange, an ad hoc consortium from Ontario colleges—was heralded by Clyde Farnsworth in the *New York Times* of June 7 as "the first time that any institution here has addressed in a substantive way the economic implications of the threatened spinoff of most of French-speaking Canada, should constitutional reform efforts collapse again, as they did last June."

Results of the symposium appear in this book under five section headings: Constitution Making; The Meech Lake Debacle; The Economics of Decentralization; Quebec and the Independence Option; and Making Federalism Work. In Section I, a group discussion with Trudeau is preceded by an introduction by McGill constitutional lawyer, Stephen A. Scott, who provides a review of the entire patriation process. The former prime minister's talk, presented verbatim with questions and answers is a *tour de force* of depth and complexity which deserves a reading by all interested Canadians. It includes a forceful argument for explicit entrenchment of sovereignty in the people rather than in their representatives in government. Also noteworthy is Trudeau's admission that he would have called a general election in 1981, if necessary, to secure a mandate, in order to declare independence for Canada unilaterally. Following this is a paper by

Michael Walker of the Fraser Institute, who spells out certain constitutional essentials.

Walker agrees with Trudeau that popular sovereignty is a necessary characteristic for any constitution, but also calls for a constitutional convention and a referendum. He believes the people cannot be sovereign *vis-à-vis* their government without the right, within a market economy, to own and dispose of property according to rules they set for themselves under voluntary contract. Such property rights are without significance, he adds, unless the government's power to tax, spend and borrow is constitutionally restricted. In his view, a notwithstanding clause or a special status for "collective rights" is fundamentally incompatible with individual civil and economic liberty.

Journalist Andrew Coyne of the *Globe and Mail* would reject much of Canada's constitutional tradition. Condemning statism and groupism, he argues for a more individualistic form of government. The state, he says, feels it has a duty to protect Canadian identity—whatever that is—even at the cost of individual rights. Coyne argues that the highest human values enunciated in the constitution should include the market economy, and that a constitution should be drawn up by an elected convention, with its results put to a referendum.

Section II, The Meech Lake Debacle, finds the *Financial Post*'s Andrew Cohen and Eric Maldoff, founding president of the anglo-rights group Alliance Quebec, in substantial agreement over what was accomplished by the provincial premiers in 1987. Executive federalism is in disfavour—"Constitution making by stealth must go," says Cohen. Maldoff writes that Meech Lake showed an utter disregard for the people of Canada. He also raises the spectre of special powers for Quebec, charging that a deal was contrived to keep the wayward province in the confederation.

What accommodations are necessary to satisfy Quebec and save the nation? In Section III, The Economics of Decentralization, economists André Raynauld (Université de Montréal), D.A.L. Auld (Loyalist College), and Thomas Courchene (Queen's University) find much to recommend in decentralization as a means of eliminating duplication and rationalizing the Canadian economy. Courchene states it would be too costly for Quebec to opt out of the federation. He predicts that the debate over Quebec's place in the nation will soon degenerate into a battle between have and have-not provinces, in which Quebec will begin to side with those not needing continuing infusions of federal money in equalization payments. Although he is a decentralist, Courchene believes that a slowing down of the transfer system is essential. Charles Doran of Johns Hopkins University and Earl Fry of Brigham Young deal with the macroeconomics of decentralization. "Small is not beautiful in world politics," says Doran, while Fry is concerned with the numerous trade restrictions imposed by provinces (and states) in the face of the world economy's increasing globalization.

Section IV, Quebec and the Independence Option, deals mainly with the economics of breakup. The economic argument for an independent Quebec, as outlined in the notorious Bélanger-Campeau report of March 1991, does not hold up, according to the University of Western Ontario's Robert Young, and John McCallum of McGill's Department of Economics. McCallum speculates that at the moment of separation, a flight of capital from Quebec would necessarily occur, and that the free trade deal with the United States would require renegotiation—at considerable cost to Quebec and Canada. Arguing that Quebec could only separate by constitutional amendment procedures requiring consent of the rest of Canada, or by revolutionary means, Stephen Scott of McGill's Law school raises the question of legality and the use of force. It is highly unlikely, he says, that the House of Commons would authorize the breakup of Canada even if the people of Quebec desired it by referendum.

William Johnson of the Montreal *Gazette* attributes Quebec's unhappiness with Canada to a long-standing penchant by its intellectuals for scapegoating English Canada. Also concerned with mythology, David Frum of the *Wall Street Journal* speculates that the prevailing Canadian obsession with provinces joining the United States in case of breakup has no basis in reality. Losing Quebec would not mean the end of Canada, he says. McGill economist Jagdish Handa warns that Quebec might choose to go it alone because, he believes, separatism is driven by emotion and may prove stronger than any economic argument.

The final Section, Making Federalism Work, begins with an essay by another McGill economist, William G. Watson, who has much to say for preservation of the status quo. Do not drastically decentralize a prosperous and successful nation in order to keep Quebec in the fold, he advises. Preferring the separation of Quebec to substantial devolution, Watson believes that if constitutional change must come, it should be engineered by politicians—who are, after all, professionals. R.S. McCall of McGill's

Philosophy department thinks concession to an earlier constitutional idea, bilingualism by democratic choice, makes sense. American Indian leader Verna Lawrence closes the section with a warning against concessions to collectivities or leadership elites, calling tribal sovereignty in the United States a form of "American apartheid."

With the editors' final essay, the book completes a circle begun by Trudeau. It argues that the essence of a successful democratic constitution is popular sovereignty and limited government, with residual powers vested in the people. Canadian federalism is indeed imperilled: the nation is divided between founders, aboriginals, immigrants, haves and have-nots; the current constitution fails to protect private property and individual rights against an overactive state; taxing, spending and borrowing are unrestricted; and the Bank of Canada is dangerously exposed to political demands for inflationary easy money. In the editors' opinion, some of these failings are correctible through the most recent proposals for constitutional reform. Ominously, others remain to be addressed.

Section I

Constitution Making

Canada's Constitution of 1982: Historical Background

Stephen A. Scott

The following was given as an introduction to Pierre Trudeau's discussion with the members of the symposium.

Canada under the British North America Act

FROM THE 1920S, AND PARTICULARLY the 1930s, Canada functioned for most practical purposes as an independent sovereign state, and increasingly was recognised as such by the international community. In terms of its constitutional law, however, it remained part of the Empire.

Prior to the Statute of Westminster in 1931, the British parliament had an absolute and unlimited legislative sovereignty with respect to Canada and all aspects of its constitutional and legal system. This power was decreasingly exercised as a matter of practice; the Parliament of Canada and the legislatures of the Canadian provinces had both legally and practically a very wide freedom of legislation. Nonetheless, they could not legislate inconsistently with any Imperial Act extending to Canada either by express words or by necessary implication. The Statute of Westminster in 1931 changed both these principles or rules, up to a point. The Parliament of Canada and the provincial legislatures were now allowed to make laws inconsistent with an Imperial Act extending to Canada. Further, The Statute of Westminster provided that no future Imperial Act would extend to Canada as part of its law unless its terms declared that "the Dominion" had requested and consented to it. The British Parliament could declare that any particular Act was enacted with the request and consent of "the Dominion." This appeared to mean the federal legislative institutions, or at least the federal executive, the provinces having nothing to do with making a request or giving consent even if they were to be affected by the Imperial Act in question. The Act would extend to Canada as long as Westminster framed it with words declaring Canada's request and consent. To that extent, Canada's increased sovereignty depended on British good will.

From this you might suppose that, a few technicalities aside, the imperial legislative supremacy had been removed by the Statute of Westminster. However, there was a crucial overriding provision: nothing in the Statute extended to the amendment of the British North America Acts, 1867 to 1930. Taking this proviso literally (as the Supreme Court ultimately did) meant two things. First it meant that neither the Parliament of Canada nor the provincial legislatures could enact legislation conflicting with the British North America Act. Second, the Imperial Parliament could, as a matter of strict law, enact legislation at any time with or without any request from Canada. On the other hand, since the late nineteenth century there had developed "conventional" rules—rules of "morally" obligatory constitutional practice such that the Imperial Parliament would not act to change the Canadian constitution except at the request and consent of the Dominion authorities, and in particular the request and consent of the Senate and House of Commons of Canada.

In the 50 years between 1931 and final patriation of the Constitution on April 17, 1982, there were repeated attempts to achieve the completion of Canadian legislative sovereignty by abolishing the powers of the Imperial Parliament and transferring them to a domestic Canadian amendment mechanism. This was usually envisaged as resulting from a combination— in fact, several different combinations for different purposes—of federal and provincial legislative bodies, with the Sovereign completing an amendment by giving royal assent to it (as with other legislation). All of these attempts to get a consensus failed, most notably the attempts in the 1950s and early 1960s by Prime Minister Diefenbaker to devise and enact the Fulton-Favreau formula. He came close to success, but Quebec at the last minute withdrew its consent.

The Trudeau Initiative, 1980-1982

Our immediate story begins with Prime Minister Trudeau's constitutional initiative in October 1980. At that time, the Imperial Parliament's residual constitutional supremacy under the Statute of Westminster remained. What had been given with one hand in 1931 had simultaneously been taken back with the other since, as we have seen, the Imperial Parliament retained *de jure* the full and unfettered power to amend our constitutional enactments in any way it wished. We in Canada had never been able to agree on a new law-making process which would replace the Westminster Parliament as master of the constitution.

In October 1980, Mr. Trudeau's government proposed a draft constitutional text with more or less the scope of the reform which finally became the 1982 Act, but with quite different terms. It contained an amending formula known as the Victoria scheme, basically requiring the consent of Quebec, Ontario, two Maritime provinces and two western provinces for a proposed constitutional amendment to become law. However, Mr. Trudeau's proposal did provide a way of getting around the need for the provincial legislative assemblies to pass amendments. It provided for a referendum mechanism, the referendum to be held if so ordered by the federal authorities. If there was a national majority in the referendum, and also majorities in the grouping of provinces necessary to pass an amendment, then the amendment would become law with or without the approval of the provincial legislative assemblies. Mr. Trudeau's proposal also contained a charter of rights (without what has become known as the override or notwithstanding clause which allows Parliament and any provincial legislature to opt out of most of the guarantees of fundamental rights in respect of any particular statute). The draft, as Mr. Trudeau's government proposed it, was a request by the House of Commons and the Senate to the Parliament at Westminster to enact this scheme. The British parliament was to be asked to act for the last time: to transfer, and end, its own powers. The proposal was intended by Mr. Trudeau to proceed to Westminster with or without the approval of the provincial legislative assemblies.

Opposition and Resistance

This scheme immediately encountered opposition and resistance, one might say of the most sustained and bitter character, from the opposition parties in the federal parliament, particularly the Progressive Conservatives, and also from eight of the ten provincial governments, that is to say all except Ontario and New Brunswick. Resistance focused in part on the proposed curtailment of provincial sovereignty by the imposition of an entrenched charter of rights. The referendum element in the amendment process, however, attracted the most envenomed reaction.

A special joint committee of the Senate and House of Commons was appointed to consider the draft. It reported on February 13, 1981, proposing a variety of changes. A number of compromises had secured the (rather unenthusiastic) concurrence of the Federal New Democratic Party and most of its MPs. Nevertheless, the revised draft met nearly the same obstruction in the House of Commons as the original proposal of October 1980.

Only on April 8, 1981—with no end to the debate in sight—was all-party agreement on procedure announced in the House of Commons. Under this agreement a special order of the House was unanimously adopted, fixing a timetable for the disposition by the House of all amendments to the text reported from the committee and, ultimately, for the disposition of the final text as it might (or might not) be amended by the House. This agreement, however, also committed the government to await the judgment of the Supreme Court of Canada on pending appeals from decisions of the Manitoba, Newfoundland and Quebec Courts of Appeal on questions referred to them by the governments of these provinces. At issue were both the constitutional propriety and the legal validity (or legal consequences) of the course of action upon which the federal Houses had embarked.

The Supreme Court of Canada's majority decision of September 28, 1981, in what is often called the Patriation Reference, held that as a matter of law the authority of the British parliament survived intact and unimpaired; that is to say, it could validly and effectively legislate on the Canadian constitution, either on its own initiative or in response to any request. But the Court also held that extra-legal "conventions" existed, rendering constitutionally improper a federal parliamentary request to Westminster directly affecting the provinces' constitutional position, without sufficient provincial consensus. Moreover, whatever the "necessary" consensus might be, the two provinces of Ontario and New Brunswick did not suffice (unanimity, however, was not required).

Even if it had remained politically possible for federal parliamentary majorities to force the measure as it then stood through both Houses of the Canadian Parliament (amendments were approved by the House of Commons on April 23, 1981, and by the Senate on April 24, 1981), it was doubtful that the Government in the United Kingdom would (or even could) carry a bill in the terms requested through the parliament at Westminster. (Well-informed friends in Britain assured me that it would not have been possible for Mrs. Thatcher's Government to force it through Parliament after the Supreme Court's decision on the Patriation Reference. The Labour Party doesn't like bills of rights, while the Conservative backbench would have accepted the view of "their friends in Alberta" and elsewhere in Canada that the process was unfair.)

The Negotiated Solution

A negotiated solution thus became the only alternative. This was achieved on November 5, 1981, the signatories being the executive governments of Canada and of all provinces save Quebec. The agreed scheme was based largely on an earlier interprovincial agreement of April 16, 1981 (the so-called April Accord) among the eight opposing provincial governments. In particular, the federal-provincial agreement of November 5, 1981, introduced the legislative override (reflected in Section 33 of the Constitution Act, 1982) allowing the Parliament of Canada and the provincial legislatures to override, by express statutory language, most of the guarantees of the Canadian Charter of Rights and Freedoms. It also adopted from the April Accord, a scheme of constitutional amending formulae which Prime Minister Trudeau had repeatedly denounced as tending to create a "checkerboard Canada." These amending procedures, based on the so-called Vancouver model, had, and have, almost no resemblance on essential points to the federal proposals which they displaced.

On November 18, 1981, the Minister of Justice accordingly introduced into the House of Commons a resolution for a joint address to the Sovereign conforming to the federal-provincial agreement. Further changes had indeed been made in order to accommodate positions adopted by the government of Quebec. For example, Section 23(1)(a) of the Constitution Act,

1982, guarantees to Canadian citizens of English or French mother tongue, in any province in which they are the linguistic minority, a primary and secondary school education in their mother tongue for their children. It is not in force in Quebec, and cannot be brought into force there without the consent either of Quebec's executive government or of its legislature (the National Assembly). This was one further concession to Quebec made after November 5, 1981. Nevertheless, it proved impossible to secure that province's agreement to the project. Indeed, Quebec began to escalate its demands beyond its bargaining position as part of the eight-province common front. Quebec has remained opposed, as a matter of principle, to the ultimate Canada Act and has not accepted the issue as settled politically—even though, as Premier René Lévesque had said on several occasions (including November 5, 1981) there were only three issues outstanding:

(1) the (partial) entrenchment of the minority-language educational guarantee;

(2) the entrenchment of the "mobility" guarantee;

(3) compensation to provinces exercising their powers to opt out of certain constitutional amendments.

On December 2, 1981, the House of Commons of Canada adopted the final text of the constitutional proposals, and on December 8, 1981, the Senate of Canada followed suit. The Bill to give them effect was passed by both houses of the British parliament, and received royal assent on March 29, 1982, becoming law as the Canada Act, 1982—the ultimate exercise of imperial legislative authority over Canada. Scheduled to the Canada Act and forming an integral part of it was the Constitution Act, 1982, which contained most of the substance of the reforms. The majority of the provisions of these enactments came into operation on April 17, 1982, with the Queen's proclamation made that day in Ottawa.

It is worth adding that in December 1982, the Supreme Court of Canada gave judgment in a second Patriation Reference, brought by Quebec. As the Court pointed out, the 1982 reforms were now, as a matter of law, valid and effective according to their terms everywhere in Canada—including Quebec—regardless of whether the conventions had been respected (note that in legal terms, Quebec was fully bound by and part of the constitution, including the 1982 reform, and did not have to be "brought back" into it). But the Court consented to rule on the extra-legal question of whether the patriation process had indeed respected the relevant conventions although this could of course have no legal consequences one way or the other. The Court reiterated its previous position that a sufficient provincial consensus, but not provincial unanimity, had been required by conventions whenever the federal authorities proposed to approach Westminster with a request for legislation directly affecting provincial rights and powers. Furthermore, the Court added, Quebec had no special entitlement to a "conventional" veto of its own. It followed (in the Court's view) that the nine other provinces' consent to the 1982 reforms had sufficed to respect the conventions, and thus Quebec's rights had not been violated—either as a matter of law or as a matter of constitutional practice—by the 1982 patriation process.

Constituent Power, Sovereignty and the Constitution

Pierre Elliott Trudeau

The following is taken from the transcript of the discussion between former prime minister Pierre Trudeau and members of the symposium.

Mr. Trudeau: I'm glad we began with that introduction [by Stephen Scott, see previous essay] because everything else from now on will seem simple.

A preliminary remark might consist in saying why I wrote the paper which I delivered at the Laskin Library opening in Toronto a couple of months ago. I should hasten to say it was not an attempt to cry over milk spilt by the Supreme Court, which made us come to the compromises Professor Scott described. What I was really trying to do—and I think I may have succeeded in part—was to bring to the fore the question of sovereignty in Canada and whether its locus rested in the federal government or in the provinces or in a combination of both, or whether it rested, as I held, in the Canadian people. I don't know if I have succeeded in that, but I think you will all agree that it is important that that question be debated here and in many other places. Otherwise, we will never have a clear notion of what or who the constituent power is or was in Canada, and therefore what sovereignty exactly means.

Popular Sovereignty vs. Compact Theory

I'm talking sovereignty, of course, in the Augustinian sense which Professor Irving Brecher and I were discussing just before we sat down. That seems to be quite misunderstood by those who talk about sovereignty-association as though Quebec could be fully sovereign and yet share its sovereignty with the rest of Canada in some undefined way which would lead to some kind of special status, or distinct society.

As I pointed out in the paper, the Supreme Court—fatally I think—tilted in the direction of the Compact Theory, in the sense that its judgment said that the people were not sovereign but that the constituent power (the locus of sovereignty) rested in some undefined combination of the federal and a certain number of provincial governments' consent. This was a proposition that I had tried to get away from in our draft joint address put to Parliament in October 1980.

Professor Scott reminded us of something generally forgotten in the debate, which is that we had introduced a notion that sovereignty ultimately resided in the people. First we did that by having a charter of rights that said—what is the way Jefferson put it, you just quoted to me?

Tom Velk: A bill of rights is what every people in the world are entitled to against every government.

Mr. Trudeau: Exactly. And if the people are entitled against the government, it means that they have the final say. Therefore, in our Charter of Rights and Freedoms, that's exactly what we were trying to do. That's why we called it the "people's package," as opposed to the government's package, which was to come later. We were saying sovereignty rested there and governments couldn't do certain things, which were the list of inalienable rights. Also important: we put in the amending formula provision, which in a sense is another way of defining the constituent power. We also put in a last resort deadlock-breaking mechanism for when the provinces and the federal government could not agree. We said, "Well, let's go to the people." Though that may or may not have been frequently used it was something the provinces shied away from in horror, including two provinces that went along with us, Ontario and New Brunswick. There was perhaps less horror in their case but they didn't like the idea and as soon as we had to give up something in the negotiation, that is what they suggested we give up.

So the importance of defining sovereignty was central to our proposal, but it was not discussed in front of the Supreme Court as such. When the Supreme Court rendered its judgment it made no direct reference to the notion, though of course its judgment implied that sovereignty was exercised by a combination of federal and provincial powers.

The Supreme Court and the Amending Formula

With the amending formula we have now, which as Professor Scott said was the result of the compromise reached in the fall of 1981, we are stuck with something that says the people are not involved in the amending process but the provinces and the federal government, as entities, are. I guess we see the consequences of that in the Meech Lake approach, which was the most recent attempt to change some fundamentals of the constitution, and which failed. But the attempt shows that in the premiers' minds and, I daresay, in political scientists' and most legal minds, that is the way things were done. The people who saved us from that were precisely the people who had got used to the notion of a Charter, and who instinctively sensed that they were more important than governments. And I guess it's generally recognized that if Meech Lake failed it's because the people were not involved.

So the object of my doing that speech, apart from rendering homage to a great jurist and a personal friend, Bora Laskin, was to try to resuscitate discussion around the notion of sovereignty. So far as I know, I haven't succeeded much. There have been a couple of seminars like this where we got to the subject. I have to confess I don't know too much about the literature currently written, but I did receive clippings of Marcel Adam, who as far as I know is the only journalist—and perhaps the only person— who wrote about my Toronto text from that point of view, which I think is the most important point of view.

Am I right? I haven't, as I say, read too many of the learned journals. But am I right in saying that the speech, if it caused any comment at all, was more about an *obiter dicta*, an ad lib where I talked about sorcerer's apprentices rather than about the content itself? Which is my fault because I learned a long while ago in politics that you shouldn't scoop yourself. If you've got a text, you should stick to the text because not all journalists, like Marcel Adam, go to the heart of the matter. They usually take the easy quote, though I shouldn't fall into that foible either.

On the judgment itself, just one word. I'm not crying over spilt milk, though I do think the judgment is not a good one. Of all the many reasons I gave in the speech I think one stands out first and foremost, and that is the judges wanted to find a convention. Now convention, according to Dicey and all those who have since written about it, is something which arises from precedents created by political practices. Therefore what the Supreme Court did was look at the 22 times the BNA Act had been amended by the U.K. on a request of the Canadian parliament. Of those 22 occasions it looked at five and, having looked at five, it said there is a convention that when amendments affecting the distribution of powers are proposed, they call for unanimous consent of the provinces. This indeed is what the five precedents said. In 1930, 1931, 1940, 1951, and 1964 there was unanimous consent of the provinces. But my paper goes on to say our 1981 amendment was not at all of the same nature; it wasn't redistributing powers, it was just taking powers equally from both federal and provincial governments.

But apart from all those arguments it seems to me there is one which indicates that the Supreme Court decision was fatally flawed. It is that having found a convention of unanimous provincial consent—having retained these five precedents of unanimous consent—they went on to invent a convention which said substantial consent is enough. Now there were no precedents for substantial consent and of the eight provinces pleading before them none had alleged that, except for Saskatchewan. They invented a precedent of substantial consent. As Eugene Forsey, whom I quote in the paper, said after having meted out this rule to the federal government, the federal prime minister didn't know whether he had to go for five, six, seven, eight, or nine provinces to have that substantial consent. So you could hardly say that a convention exists when it cannot be defined even by the courts that proposed to have found it.

On the legal, conventional side, that seems to me the most crippling argument of the judgment. But I repeat again, and I hope the discussion will bear me out, the main question is, Where is sovereignty? We certainly lost the first round in 1982 of establishing sovereignty in the people. We lost it courtesy of the Supreme Court. But we didn't quite lose it with the people, because of their interest in the Charter—weakened, as Professor Scott again reminded us, by the fact there is a notwithstanding clause that in certain cases, not all, permits the provinces to overturn a provision of the Charter, controlled by the Court.

I guess that's enough to let the debate begin.

The Override Clause and the Charter

Irving Brecher: I am very pleased that this issue, sovereignty, is now really coming to the fore. I think that it is important, not only in a Canadian context, but in the international context. On the domestic front, one question that comes up in my mind is the notwithstanding clause. I'd be very interested to know what your basic position has been and is on its merits.

And then as a second, perhaps more general question: how do you feel about the way in which the Charter of Rights, which you were so instrumental in providing, has been interpreted by the Courts over these past ten years? Do you feel that what you were looking for in the Charter has been interpreted in ways that you think are on the whole positive and reinforce this notion that sovereignty rests in the people?

Mr. Trudeau: On the first point, I certainly felt that the notion of the override clause is fundamentally contradictory to the notion of inalienable rights resting with the people. I was convinced that Section 1—which permits the Supreme Court to do the equivalent of what the American Supreme Court does *motu proprio* [of its own accord]—can limit the right of free speech to cry "Fire!" in a crowded theatre, as Justice Holmes put it. In our case the courts can limit the exercise of free speech or any other freedom, but only after the burden has been placed on the legislature to demonstrate that it is acceptable in a democratic and free society. So I thought that Section 1 gave the courts enough latitude to prevent the abuse of the black letter of the law in applying the fundamental rights and freedoms.

I know there are other minds who believe that the notwithstanding clause is an improvement. As a matter of fact, I heard a very good *exposé* here at one of your meetings—I think it was law professor Lorraine Weinrib from Toronto. She makes an interesting case that the notwithstanding clause is a compromise. It permits us to have a Charter but then puts in the possibility for the provinces or the federal government to override the Charter, although they must justify doing so. I don't agree with that. I think the Charter is fundamentally flawed because of the override clause. I could have gotten rid of the compromise, of the notwithstanding clause, by getting rid of the Charter. That was quite clear to us in these negotiations imposed on us by the Supreme Court. And I had to ask myself, Well, will it be easier sometime in the future to get a full-blown Charter without any compromise clause, any notwithstanding clause, or will it be easier to have a full-blown Charter, flawed with the notwithstanding clause, which pressure of the people—of the electorate on their government—would be able to get rid of someday in the future? And I came to the conclusion that it would be much harder to come back someday with our amending formula to get all provinces to accept the Charter unflawed. That's how the choice was made. But I still hope that in the future we will be able to get rid of that clause. As education of the people proceeds on the notion of fundamental values that everyone shares, it is not inconceivable that that will happen.

On your second question I must say that the courts in general and the legal profession, not always for altruistic reasons, have made great use of the Charter, and I think the Supreme Court has been superb in giving life to the Charter. If it weren't for the bench and the bar I don't think we'd have the awareness that we have today in Canada of this notion of popular sovereignty, that the people do have rights over and above the power of government. Having criticized those members of the bench that had arrived at a majority judgment in 1981, I have to say that while many of those same judges have not atoned, because I don't think they feel they have sinned, in my mind they have certainly done a great job in giving life to the Charter.

Jagdish Handa: Within this country, people assume there are two different societies or cultures or nations. The notwithstanding clause is one way of expressing that division. A single majority rule would not have served this country. Other countries which tried to adopt it—and one can think of Cyprus or Ireland—repeatedly show that when you have a very significant percentage of the population that feels itself to be different from the others, that portion will not accept such rules.

Mr. Trudeau: Of course, your point holds true in unitary states with or without constitutional government. If you look at Northern Ireland or perhaps even Scotland, they wouldn't be more happy with majority rule in Westminster; nor would some of the irredentists from the French Basque country or Brittany, although they have a charter and a reasonably good one in France. So your question is a good one, but the question is where is the best answer? We proposed in 1980 that the deadlock-breaking mechanism be a referendum, but one voted on by the four great regions of Canada, which in a sense gave a pretty good guarantee to the province where the majority of French people were. It gave a pretty good guarantee to those various minorities which exist in the West, which certainly could band together to protect their rights. Therefore we didn't need a notwithstanding clause if, paradoxically enough, the Victoria formula had not been rejected by Mr. Bourassa in Victoria back in 1971—the very Bourassa who is asking for a veto power now rejected it in 1971—and had it not been rejected by Mr. Lévesque at the Gang of Eight meeting in April 1981, and again by the same people who rejected it when we proposed it in the House of Commons. That was our preferred amending formula, which gave some kind of protection and gave life in a sense to the notion of federalism. So don't blame us.

Compact Theory and the Right to Secede

John McCallum: If I understand correctly, you're saying that the Compact Theory may not have won the war but has won a couple of battles, suggesting that a lot of the sovereignty today does in fact reside in the provinces. So I would like to ask what this implies—it would seem to me it implies something—for the right of a given province to secede if it so desires, in terms of both legality and legitimacy. Because if the Compact Theory is right, does that not imply they came together voluntarily and may disperse if any one wishes to, with due notice and proper democratic procedures?

Mr. Trudeau: I have to answer, like the Red Queen, that the Compact Theory means what you want it to mean. I think historically it did not mean the right to secede. So far as I know, the first time it was invoked in the context of constitutional debates was in 1927 when Premier Ferguson of Ontario and Premier Taschereau of Quebec invoked the Compact Theory in order to frustrate Mackenzie King's attempt to find an amending formula to try to patriate our constitution. I think it would be unfair to suspect either Premier Ferguson or Premier Taschereau or their peoples in those days of wanting to invoke it in order to secede. Therefore it doesn't necessarily follow from the Compact Theory that you must secede. But as time went on, I guess, we awakened to the notion of separatism in Quebec, which had just been unthinkable before the Quiet Revolution in the sense that Quebec had nowhere to go, really couldn't govern itself as a modern state, and didn't want to. But after 1960 the Quiet Revolution gave Quebec the tools to govern itself as a modern, independent state and therefore the option of the Compact Theory—meaning full sovereignty to each of the constituent parts, or at least to that part of the two nations, if we believed in the two nations—became a reality.

Incidentally, this permits me to tell Professor McCallum obliquely that he quite correctly says that my own thinking on Compact Theory was rather loose and imprecise until more recently. He is quite right. I don't think anyone felt the need. That is why in my speech I talked about how there exists, to my knowledge, no contemporary doctrine of Canadian sovereignty. I think that until the Quiet Revolution there was a general notion that sovereignty was exercised by some combination of the federal government and the provinces. This would lead us to believe there is some kind of a Compact Theory, at least at the historical origins of the constitution of Canadian Confederation. But I never held that this was a true compact. Jurisprudence and many politicians talk about the notion of a pact, whether it be between founding peoples or four founding colonies or whatever. But I think everybody says: That is how it started, but what exists is the law of the Imperial Parliament telling its colonies that they are a country. It was less relevant in those days because nobody talked of separation. But now that we're not only talking of separation but the provinces themselves have articulated it—as Premier Blakeney did in some of our discussions and as Mr. Joe Clark, then leader of the Opposition, articulated in his opposition to our patriation address—the notion of Compact Theory is much more founded in political reality and, in a certain sense, in the judgment of the Court.

Having answered the first question that way I don't think I can answer the second: What is needed to make separation of one province from Canada real and democratic? I think you would find most politicians—I don't know about academia—have said we're not going to go to war if one province like Quebec wants to separate. We will respect the will of the people. I think that reflects a Canadian distaste for violent solutions. But it really doesn't solve the nitty-gritty problems of what will happen if a province votes in some democratic way to separate. Because all kinds of questions arise.

I was asked this question at the time of the patriation process by journalists in Washington and they were all shocked that I wouldn't do like Abraham Lincoln and call out the troops. I said: Look, I have not been elected in any of my mandates to deal with the problem of a province separating. Therefore I have no authority either to call out the troops or to support or to negotiate, and I think there would have to be at least an election of a new government in order to decide whether they're going to call out the troops or negotiate, and what the negotiation would be. But I suspect that when you get closer to the real point—when it's a hypothesis that becomes a reality—there'll be all sorts of monkey wrenches thrown into the works, not only of an economic kind but of a substantial kind. If it is all right for Quebec to separate from Canada, why wouldn't it be all right for the Inuit to separate from Quebec? Or for that matter for everybody west of St. Lawrence Boulevard up to and including the Ottawa River or somewhere in Temiskaming—who would have voted, presumably, against separation—to separate from the new country and become part of Canada? So I think it's a dog's breakfast and it isn't susceptible to rational debate at this point.

But it should not escape completely those who are seriously talking of separation. When I discuss this, they say the Constitution gives defined frontiers to Quebec, so that will be the frontier of Quebec when it separates. Which is a curious non sequitur because how can you invoke the constitution once you have separated from the country that bound you by the constitution to be part of it? The thing is even more complex due to the fact that, if we are logical, the borders of Quebec include minorities just as the borders of Ontario and New Brunswick include minorities, in one case English and in the other case French. So maybe the right of self-determination of a people should be voted on by all French Canadians to bind them into whatever parts of northern Ontario and central Quebec and western New Brunswick, rather than this mishmash of peoples in Quebec which has a majority of French-speaking people but a dwindling minority—I think barely a plurality—of "true *Québécois*," if you permit the enormity of the suggestion.

A Constitution by Referendum?

William Watson: We are all agreed that the people are sovereign, though we have some difficulty agreeing on what that means. In 1981, why didn't you consult the people in a referendum and then simply go to Westminster and say, Look, we got a 50 per cent vote, we won in all regions—do it?
Mr. Trudeau: There are two answers. One is that I did propose it as my own deadlock-breaking mechanism. It is one I had in mind for quite a bit of time before the final November 1981 conferences. And you may recall that I did

propose it at one point to the assembled premiers when I saw we were getting nowhere and the thing was going to fail. I proposed the following scheme: since nobody could say we don't want to have our own constitution, we would patriate exactly the BNA Act, as it was, but we would give ourselves three years to try and agree on *(a)* a charter of rights and *(b)* an amending formula. Of course, the Charter of Rights was mine and the amending formula was the Victoria formula, which was also ours. It would give the provinces maybe three years to try and sell to us or to the people their Vancouver charter (as it was correctly called by Professor Scott, even though it was invented at Edmonton at a previous meeting of the premiers, the Gang of Eight). If after three years there hadn't been agreement we would have gone to the people with the question, Do you want a charter of rights or not, and do you want the Victoria formula as opposed to the Vancouver formula?

I can't pretend it would have been an easy debate but it certainly would have been easy to win on the Charter, because most of the provinces have charters of their own and they didn't see themselves easily campaigning against a charter for Canadians. The amending formula would have been more complex, and I must say I am not that crazy about putting that kind of question to the people. But I was ready to do it rather than face complete failure. That is what I proposed to Premier Lévesque and what he accepted and what split the Gang of Eight, because the seven other premiers really didn't like referenda—they knew they would lose the referendum on the Charter and they were far from sure they would win one on the amending formula, so they would rather compromise. And you know the story after that. Lévesque said the question was too complicated and he changed his mind, but by then the Gang of Eight had been broken apart. But I didn't do it really just in terms of Napoleon at Austerlitz—you know, splitting the enemy. I did it because I thought it was one solution. The other answer to your question, of course, is that by then the Supreme Court had given us an amending formula. What you're asking is: Why didn't I go to London? It would have made a hell of a nice campaign.

William Watson: How about earlier? Instead of appealing to the Supreme Court, why not appeal to the people?

Mr. Trudeau: I didn't appeal to the Supreme Court. I appealed, I guess, to the remnants of the Compact Theory in order to bring in the sovereignty-of-the-people theory. I was using what has always been done, a joint address of both Houses, to get a constitution which would permit me to say: Hereafter we will need the people to break the deadlock. But when the provinces early in the game appealed to the Supreme Court I surely couldn't say: I'm not going to wait for their judgment and I will go to Britain, maybe with no legal mandate. Once I had the legal mandate I don't think Britain would have opposed it. Let me ask Stephen Scott: What would your informants have said to that?

Stephen Scott: The question I asked them was not based on the assumption that you had fought and won a referendum here. I suspect that if you had had substantial majorities and the polls indicated you had majority support even in Quebec that might have made a difference. The view I had was that it was out of the question for Mrs. Thatcher to go with a three-line whip, using all her political capital to force reluctant Tory MPs who had friends in Alberta and all over the place to toe the line on a matter of no political interest to her.

Mr. Trudeau: On that, it is interesting to note that Mrs. Thatcher had given me her unequivocal word that if I came for patriation with a joint address by the Parliament of Canada she would have no choice, because she believed above all in the sovereignty of Parliament and therefore if the Parliament of Canada—

Stephen Scott: Was this before or after the Supreme Court judgment?

Mr. Trudeau: This was well before. It was in June of 1980 and then she repeated it again at the Commonwealth meeting in Melbourne right after the Supreme Court judgment.

Stephen Scott: Oh, she repeated it after the Supreme Court judgment?

Mr. Trudeau: In private. But she would have stuck to her word, I know that. Maybe she wouldn't have put the three-line whip on and maybe I would have had trouble, but I think she was astute enough to remember the Rhodesia problem and the UDI (unilateral declaration of independence) problem. We're all in historical might-have-beens here. I don't think I would even have had to go for a referendum. Maybe I would have, I don't know. But it would have been interesting after that last meeting in November with the provinces, had they refused to accept a charter and an amending formula which in reality gave the veto to the four regions. It would have been interesting to see if I couldn't have won an election on that and told the British parliament: Look, you better get on with it because my election is on Canadian independence. Now, this sounds a little like *pétage de bretelles*, as we say in French, when you pull your suspenders and let them snap back, so I don't know what would have happened. But anybody can speculate. I think the British were sufficiently concerned with the possibility of UDI that at some point they would have had to move. Otherwise we would have had UDI.

Now would I have had support in that kind of election? Maybe not. Mackenzie King won it in 1926 on a much more flimsy basis than that, but whether you could still win it in 1982, I'm not certain. I don't want to be unfair to Mrs. Thatcher. What may complicate it is that she gave me her word at a time when she—and I—didn't know exactly what would be in the patriation package. Much later, when she realized we had included a charter as well as pure patriation she might have said: Look, this isn't exactly what I meant.

Quebec and the Compact Theory

William Johnson: I was wondering whether Compact Theory could be a justification for something more general, which is hostility to the federal regime. I'm thinking particularly of the political history of ideas in Quebec, the historians' views throughout.

Mr. Trudeau: I think it is. But when you say hostility to the federal government it would mean something different than hostility to the federal regime itself. I don't think those who invoke the Compact Theory are hostile to the notion of federalism, but they want a very decentralized, loose confederation, a community of communities as Mr. Clark used to call it—a confederation of shopping centres as I used to call it. Obviously, there is hostility to a strong federal government and that is more or less implicit in the Compact theorists going back to Premier Ferguson of Ontario, and it probably would still be true today. Ontario is not afraid of a strong federal government as much as some of the other provinces are.

Decentralization

Just to go on, assuming I've understood your question, there is a fashion now—I don't know if it's waning or not—to say that the principle of subsidiarity is the one that should reign. It means you always put the power at the lowest possible level, closest to the people. That which can't be done at that level should be delegated to a higher level and so on, until you get a central government and perhaps eventually a world government. I think that's all very well for nations which have a strong historical notion of their existence as a nation. But if we're talking of new countries like Canada, I don't think you can afford to delegate *ad infinitum* to the region, thinking that the soul of Canada will be something floating up there—something the people will not know exists except in terms of taxing them—while everything else will be done on a local basis. I think it is important if you want to have a nation that it be held together by a certain number of fundamental values.

Now as you know, I am called by politicians and the media alike a centralist, *pur et dur* [dyed in the wool]. I have decentralized powers in Canada, even in the Constitution of 1982, in a way that has not ever happened before. There have been powers given to the federal government by the provinces, but I think I was the first prime minister to give powers (over indirect taxation and export of resources) to the provinces. Under my regime the fiscal powers were even further decentralized to the provinces, even beyond what they had been by the middle 1960s. I'm not trying to prove that I'm a great decentralist, but I think there is a point beyond which you cannot go. I am amused to say that Mr. Parizeau, the leader of the Parti Québécois, is constantly quoted as agreeing with me and he's told me that to my face, too. He says: You know, you and I agree on everything, that there has to be a strong central government, except I want its capital to be in Quebec City and you want it to be in Ottawa.

So I think any rational examination of Canadian federalism—which is the most decentralized federation on earth, even more than Switzerland in terms of fiscal policy—indicates that any much further drastic decentralization *à la statut particulier* [by special statute], or *société distincte* [distinct society] or *à la Chateau* consensus, which is the list of things the provinces want to decentralize, would turn Canada into a loose confederation.

Sovereignty and Secession

Tom Velk: I think there is an inconsistency between popular sovereignty and secession. It has many dimensions but one of the most obvious is one you can examine if you think about the American Civil War.

Without a sense of popular sovereignty you don't have a good reason to prevent a secession aimed at reducing or suppressing liberties, which is the only kind of secession that is dangerous.

Mr. Trudeau: My own comment on your comment is that if you look at the Civil War there are some parallels. We all recall that the southern states were, I think, justifiably complaining that they were paying more to the North than they were getting back—this was before the days of social security and shared cost programs, and the wealth of the South was flowing to the North. That is one of the arguments that many of the separatists make. I don't think they've founded it on good statistics yet but that is one of the arguments. But the answer of the North was to say: There is also the question of right and we are fighting to free the slaves. That is, I think, the kind of fight, in a very different context, that the federalists are waging in Quebec. Quebec is talking of the rights of the collectivity and we are talking of the rights of the individual. We are protecting the right of every individual to speak French or English to his national government and hopefully to as many provincial governments as possible, and the right of every Canadian to send his children to a French or an English school wherever he resides in Canada, with the slight tilting in favour of Quebec. But the principle is there. We are trying to vest sovereignty in the individuals, the peoples of Canada, as I think the North was in the Civil War.

Canada and Referenda

Verna Lawrence: Does the Canadian people have the right of referendum? I also want to make a comment on what you said about a referendum: You could have called a referendum.

Mr. Trudeau: Called a referendum on the patriation process?

Verna Lawrence: If it could have happened the other way, if the people could have helped you, if they could have initiated the referendum, I think you would have been very successful.

Mr. Trudeau: Well, the question is a contemporary one because there are proposals in the Quebec legislature now to introduce a bill permitting referendums and I think there's also a question of that in the federal government, at least proposed by some of the leaders. But it is not in the law yet, and there is no tradition.

The People and the Constitution

Andrew Coyne: If, as you said, the Compact Theory is becoming more and more entrenched and if, as I'm sure you agree, it is not only inimical to popular sovereignty but fatal to the nation, it seems to me a matter of some urgency that we develop some kind of process or method to destroy it, *à la* constitutional convention or something like that. Is there any way to force this onto the agenda? Or would you favour it?

Mr. Trudeau: I favour it in the sense of that's why I'm having this nice breakfast with you. I'm hoping the idea will begin to interest academics and media people and that it will be discussed because I think, as I said earlier, there is an instinctive support for it in the people because of their understanding of the Charter. If I were in government I suppose I would be telling the people that they are sovereign under the Charter and that they would be sovereign under something like the Victoria amending formula because if their governments didn't agree to an amendment they could support it by referendum. I think that would even be something interesting to the people of Quebec and that's why I say that when I proposed it, René Lévesque accepted it. That was his first reaction.

I didn't mean to imply the Compact Theory is getting more and more accepted. I think it has always been accepted in some form or other. It has generally been debunked by the legal minds who say: Look, whatever the discussions were before and whatever the idea behind Canada, now we have a constitution—in the first case the BNA Act and now the Canada Act. But politicians, I guess a majority of them, have always preferred the Compact Theory and they probably still do. I don't think it's getting worse. I think the intellectual vacuum in which the Supreme Court made its judgment is still there, and apart from Marcel Adam I don't know anybody who is beginning to raise the question in serious terms, as he did in referring in quite a lengthy way to the American views of sovereignty at the time of the Civil War.

Morton Weinfeld: A referendum is a kind of ratification process after a deal has been worked out and is on the table. Are you in favour, as the last questioner has suggested, of a constitutional convention or a constituent assembly? The counter-example that is sometimes raised is the example of the American Constitution that was drafted in a hot summer by 55 upper-class white males.

Mr. Trudeau: When I was prime minister, people who were fed up with endless federal-provincial meetings did propose both publicly and privately that we appoint a group of wise men who could solve the problem. It always offended me when I was prime minister to think that a constituent assembly by any other name could do better than what the politicians were doing. But of course I was a politician in those days and I was in power, so I was obviously a bit prejudiced—I have to say that. I would imagine today's politicians would have the same reaction: "Look, we were elected. Sure, there may be a lot of wise people. We can get them to give their views to the Spicer Committee or the Beaudoin Committee or whatever else, but *we* are the ones who are elected to decide."

Now I wouldn't be giving the same answer if, as in the case of the United States, we had won our independence as a result of a revolution. That's a different situation. There was no longer any sovereignty; it had been in the Imperial Parliament, and then it was overthrown by the force of arms. Therefore the people had to get together and decide how they are going to govern themselves. That is why a constituent assembly was the only resort short of some dictatorial assumption of power by General Washington or someone, which would have been contrary to the whole spirit of the debates leading to the Revolutionary War. So the American case cannot be applied to Canada because we assumed sovereignty over a very long process. We took it from the United Kingdom first by the Statute of Westminster and then finally by the Canada Act of 1982. There are governing powers here, founded on what we know to be the people's will, i.e., the elections. There is no tradition of referenda, as I was telling one of the participants, and therefore there is also no tradition of constituent power. I believe the people should act as sovereign people and as Jefferson put it, the best way to correct them if they are misinformed is to educate them. Hence my modest participation in the process of educating the people and the elites, the leaders, to the notion that we have to discuss sovereignty.

Eric Maldoff: As I understand sovereignty as put forward by you today, Prime Minister, you are referring to the sovereignty of the people to have their rights, to be able to communicate with their government, to be able to educate their children. Once we agree with sovereignty, how do you get people to have confidence in the system—that the sovereignty of the people will not be used to undermine the sovereignty of the individual or the minority?

Mr. Trudeau: Well, I guess my quick answer is the one I gave to the *Club des cent*, a group of French-speaking professionals between 25 and 35 which was asking that kind of question two months ago. I said: Well, look at the

European Community. Take France, for instance; in the Parliament of the Community at Strasbourg, it is retaining something like 18 per cent of its sovereignty. The rest of it is shared with Germany and Italy and the rest of the Community. How will the individual be protected in the European Community? The French obviously think they are living in a democratic environment and that certain basic principles will be respected, like that of permitting each country to protect its identity in whatever way it feels desirable. But many of the institutions, mainly economic but also political, will be delegated eventually to some higher power. That is federalism, my friend. There is an element of trust, of course. I think it's hard to argue that, at least in recent times, that trust has been misplaced in the case of Quebeckers. I don't think Quebeckers are a persecuted people, though admittedly in the early years of Confederation they were the object of many, many injustices: Ontario, New Brunswick, the West, the Riel Affair, the rules of education and so on. I always argue with my French-speaking Quebec colleagues that if the anglos are the enemy, they are not very fearsome and they are not very strong because we certainly have a great deal of control over our fate in Quebec. And ever since the Quiet Revolution, when we decided to become modern, nobody prevented us from becoming modern. It's hard to look at any period of history when, for any substantial period of time, French Canadians have been without influence in Ottawa. Therefore I say, sure, it would be safer to be independent but that is not the way of progress. You have to take some risks, and are the risks very great by belonging to this Confederation?

Of course, that's the theoretical answer but in practice your question is met with all sorts of difficult sub-questions. Who is sovereign in this particular case? Is it the Quebec people which include, as we know, a lot of minorities, English-speaking and otherwise? Or is it French Canadians? And who has authority to speak for the French Canadians? Why is it Quebec rather than Ottawa? Because historically, in recent years, with bilingualism and the CBC and Radio-Canada and l'Office du Film [National Film Board] and the Conseil des Arts [Canada Council], the French language has been probably protected more by Ottawa than by Quebec. That's beginning to change now and doubts are being cast on the very notion of bilingualism and so on by people who should know better. The French in Canada include not only those who live in St. Tite-des-Caps but they include those who live in St. Boniface and Maillardville and other points east and west. So who speaks for whom?

Also, this notion of collectivity and individual rights: much of the defence of Quebeckers' rights is, as you know, *au nom de la collectivité* [in the name of the collectivity]. Well, our approach in the Charter was not to defend *la collectivité*, it was to defend the individuals so that they had a right to speak French and to get their governments, provincial or federal, to give them the institutions. And I'm not saying that collective action is not necessary. Of course it is. Civil society is made of trade unions, of associations of all kinds to protect rights of groups, including linguistic rights. I'm not against that. But philosophically—this is a discussion I had with Charles Taylor—I hold that rights are vested in individuals. They are not vested in collectivities. Collectivities receive them by delegation to protect the individual. But no individual is a slave to a collectivity. I can make my own history. Sure, I was born a French Canadian, but if I want to send my kids to an English school I don't see how the law can prevent me, though I see how it *does* prevent me.

That is the whole notion of the Charter. That is the inalienable right that you don't give up. We belong to a collectivity freely, but if you don't want to be part of that collectivity, you get out of it, whether it's a church or a school board or anything else. The only collectivity you can't get out of without moving physically is the state. You have to pay your taxes or you go to jail. Still, if you have a Charter of Rights, that state exercises sovereignty by delegation from the people, which gets into the social contract, though I don't want to get into that. You have to go back to really fundamental notions and I think the notion of collectivity, which is used too glibly by Quebec nationalist politicians, is a very dangerous one. I'm not saying collectivities don't have a function to play. I'm saying they should not determine the fate of individuals against their will, as was the case with the blacks in the southern states in the Civil War, and so on.

Tom Velk: I wonder if I could follow up Eric's point and ask you if some of the problem is this confusion about the idea that popular sovereignty and civil liberties mean a field of action reserved for individuals from which the state is permanently excluded. Against that there is a view of rights as some kind of capacity to call for privileges from the state, to call for benefits because you are white or black or French or English or old or young. There is a danger in that.

Mr. Trudeau: Well, I think that's a very important notion. As I said a little earlier, democracy is more than an assembly of atomistic individuals who come together to form a society. If it is only that, it risks lurching from anarchy to dictatorship. The French philosopher Maritain, and later Mounier and others, developed a notion of person and personalism that says the person is different from the individual in the sense that the person is an individual in society, and that society not only conditions him, and so on. As a democrat I believe that a strong democracy can only exist if there is a civil society; in other words, if there are a certain number of institutions between the individual and the state. The rights really go back to the individual but he is bloody well justified and perhaps prudent if he gets into groups, whether it be social clubs or trade unions or school boards or eventually municipal governments and so on, to interface between him and the state. Because we're not in Athens—the individual can't be called on to express his social needs (and perhaps even wants, though there's too many of those) all the time.

We need a civil society. And that is what is lacking in Eastern Europe, a subject I'll be discussing tomorrow in Prague. You can't go from a centrally planned government and centrally controlled economy to a market system overnight, because apart from the Communist Party—and the Communist Party was identified with the state—there was no legitimate civil society. The unions really had no power. We're getting into an interesting subject of political philosophy here but I want to make it clear that, when I say that popular sovereignty emerges from the people, you can have all kinds of interpretations of the social contract, as there have been all kinds of interpretations of Rousseau's social contract. Maybe it is the formula for dictatorship. Maybe it is the formula for anarchy or something in between. We're talking now in the tradition of some centuries of democracy in the West and I think we begin to know what it means.

Constitutional Essentials: Popular Sovereignty, Property Rights, Tax and Deficit Limitations, and Individual Liberty

Michael A. Walker

Individual Sovereignty and Constitutional Change

I WAS BORN IN NEWFOUNDLAND. I mention that because I was born at a time when that country was not a part of Canada. When I left in the early 1960s to go to Nova Scotia to attend university, my grandfather was deeply saddened because he was a Newfoundland nationalist who harboured deep misgivings about Canada. The fact that he decried the union with Canada in spite of the fact that he was incomparably better off than he would have been otherwise gave me an early taste for how powerful are the emotions which attach to nationalism—in spite of their economic costs.

Not much has changed. Premier Clyde Wells was instrumental in stopping the Meech Lake Accord. In spite of the fact that in the resulting turmoil Newfoundland's flow of transfer payments would almost certainly be placed in jeopardy, Wells was regarded as triumphant (over the "Canadian Wolf," to use the term by which Canada was described in a popular anti-confederation song in the late 1940s) and accorded a hero's welcome when he returned to Newfoundland. The cost to the average Newfoundlander if the system of interregional transfers was to collapse would be $3,095, or roughly ten times the loss to the average Quebecker from the cessation of net federal transfers.

So I think we should treat these regional, or tribal or nationalist sentiments with great respect. They are obviously the stuff of which political explosives are, or can be, made.

I am delighted to be here to participate in this symposium and to discuss the relationship between individual sovereignty and the constitutional debate. The Fraser Institute has for nearly two decades been exploring how human action is expressed in the economic market place. We have constantly been made aware of the importance of the framework rules in determining how people behave, and in determining whether they are led in their private decision making to foster the development of a greater social good. We have also seen distinct signs in recent years of a deepening malaise in the polity: alienation, cynicism about democracy, a sense of loss of control over the political process, and a steady increase in tax avoidance and underground economic activity as concrete manifestations of people's unwillingness to continue to support the mechanisms of government. Along with this has come a rise in regionalist sentiment and a growing centrifugal pressure which I think are related to the other elements of discontent.

I am happy today to explore the solutions to these various problems which might be found in a focus on individual sovereignty and the market process. I agreed to come before I had done very much thinking about the specific issue I was asked to address. I must say that it has proved more challenging than I imagined. Fortunately, I think there are some solutions to be found and insights to be gained.

I found, however, that in order to think about what might emerge from a consideration of individual sovereignty I had to go pretty much back to basics and consider what sovereignty was. I apologize for the somewhat simplistic nature of this digression in such an august gathering. I also apologize for using the term sovereignty to describe individual rights under the constitution when the more usual usage is to apply the term to the state, as in the notion of sovereignty and association. I have, however, used the term deliberately to force consideration of my contention that sovereignty appropriately belongs to the people.

The Meaning of Sovereignty

Historically, all sovereignty was believed to belong to the monarch, and I suppose that is where the term sovereignty—which literally means freedom from external control—comes from. In the case of British and French traditions, rulers were believed to acquire their sovereignty via the divine right of kings.[1] Starting in the tenth or eleventh century, the ruled began to demand a limitation on the power of the king. Certainly by 1215 when the nobles extracted the Magna Carta from King John at Runneymede, the limitations on the power of the king served to convey considerable sovereignty to the people. The drawing of a line between the power of the ruler and the power of the ruled is the quintessential constitutional act. It is meant specifically to reserve certain areas of conduct which will not be subject to the dispensations of the ruler.

Sovereignty in Canada Prior to 1867

Prior to 1867, the four provinces that would be Canada had Britain and the monarch as their ruler but autonomous relationships with respect to each other. The relationship between the ruler and ruled in each of the provinces was not precisely determined and in any event was different in each of the provinces. There was no history of constitutional line drawing of the kind that had occurred in England and there was certainly no distribution of power amongst a wide group of interest groups which might, as Lord Acton noted in the case of England, restrain the power of the ruler. The rights of colonials were established in part by simply taking judicial notice of British common law, but also by virtue of the direct importation of some statute law from Britain or civil code from France.[2]

Sovereignty After 1867

The 1867 Constitution was really an act to replace Great Britain and the monarch with the federal government. The formerly independent provinces agreed to create a new government whose powers would emerge from the provinces and be determined by an agreement between them. In their own interests, the four provinces agreed to reduce their autonomy from each other and to establish a federation within which the distribution of powers between the new government they would create and themselves would accomplish a set of shared objectives (one objective, really—to secure independence from the United States). The British North America Act was therefore not a constitution in the sense of delimiting the state from the people but only in that it recorded a deal between the four founding provinces as to what measure of autonomy, as provinces, they were willing to yield in order to accomplish their goals. The only formal protections for people provided by the British North America Act were those relating to language use in the courts and legislatures and the right to maintain religious schools.[3]

Sovereignty After 1982

In 1982, the Charter of Rights and Freedoms was added to the constitution. This was meant to correct the deficiency that the original Constitution made no provisions for the written, unambiguous protection of fundamental rights. The Charter is meant to draw the line between the sovereignty of the people and the power of the state. It is meant to ensure that a parliamentary majority cannot use its legislative power to infringe the rights of some minority group. It is, in effect, intended to protect the minority from what Lord Acton, for one, called the tyranny of the majority.

Of course, in the end a super-majority (two thirds or greater, usually) will have its way and amending formulas are the formal processes by which such super-majorities can exercise whatever power they wish by amending the fundamental laws in the constitution. Nevertheless, constitutional line drawing does provide protection to minorities—at least in theory.

A Digression on Entitlements

It is important to note that the rights which are conferred by constitutional line drawing are negative rights. They are *freedoms from* rather than *entitlements to*. I raise this point because Premier Bob Rae and others have indicated that if we do reopen the constitutional bargaining, they would like to see the right to medical care, housing and other public services added to the Charter. This represents a fundamental misunderstanding of what a constitution is meant to do, since the only way positive rights of that kind can be given is if somebody else is constitutionally required to provide the resources to deliver them.

Actual Sovereignty After 1982: The Failure of the Charter

The Notwithstanding Clause

While the 1982 constitution might under some circumstances have provided a formal line limiting the power of the state and recognizing the sovereignty of ordinary citizens, in fact it did not do so. There are several reasons relating to the Charter. The first is that the Charter is deficient in terms of the provisions it contains. The second is the *non obstante* or notwithstanding clause. The omissions from the Charter will be discussed below after an exploration of the notwithstanding clause.

The result of this clause is to completely remove the inhibitory effect on the power of the majority which the Charter was meant to have. The fact that any provincial legislature may legislate, notwithstanding the provisions of Section 2 and Sections 7 to 15 of the Charter, means not only that we are open to the tyranny of the majority but also the tyranny of the minority. The government of Ontario, for example, with the support of 38 per cent of the electorate, is empowered by this clause to completely ignore the fundamental freedoms of Ontarians in laws that it passes.

There is a curious aspect of this notwithstanding clause which perhaps tells us something very profound about the Canadian psyche. In effect, this clause gives to any government the power to amend Charter provisions by a vote which, as in the case of Ontario, could constitute only 38 per cent of the population of one province; by contrast, the rest of the provisions of the constitution, which have to do with the sharing of powers between governments, require a very difficult-to-achieve approval by seven provinces representing a combination of 70 per cent of the population.

The Sovereignty Significance of Bill 178

The government of Quebec has already used the notwithstanding provision in its Bill 178 to remove the rights of some Quebeckers, and has created the fear that it may do more of the same.[4] It has also produced the political manifestation of this fear in the form of the Equality Party and discussion about how a minority might protect itself by a partitioning of the province.

The important thing about Bill 178 is the fact that it indicates to the English-speaking minority in the province of Quebec—who specifically should look to the constitution for protection from the majority—that the majority will not be bound. In fact, given the overtly populist nature of the gesture to pass this law notwithstanding the Charter provisions, and in spite of the Bill's relatively unimportant nature, the government of Quebec has illustrated precisely the problem that a constitution is designed to solve.

Recently the leader of the Bloc Québécois has been indicating that he feels Bill 178 is inappropriate. He has even used the term "repugnant" to describe it. In the context of a discussion about the fundamental rights not to be interfered with, that a constitution is supposed to convey, Mr. Bouchard has found the correct term to describe Bill 178.

The foregoing does not mean that the objective of Bill 178 was wrong or that there should be English signs. It only means that the government of Quebec chose a route to its objective that involved coercion and the prohibition of legitimate actions by its citizens. The purpose of constitutional protections is to cause us all to seek to find noncoercive means to our goals. And, in the case of Bill 178, there were clearly other ways to achieve the objective that would not have involved the violation of rights in this way. An obvious one is for the government of Quebec to use the same means it has apparently successfully used to stem the decline in the province's birth rate—financial incentives. If you place your sign in French only, we will pay you the cost of removing your existing sign and a language conversion bonus of so many dollars.[5]

The Omission of Property Rights

The 1982 constitution is also defective in that it omitted from the Charter the right to own and enjoy property, or the right to be free from legislative takings. This was a very important omission which, according to those who claim to know such things, was done to appease NDP supporters of the Liberal government.[6] If the implication is that as a matter of principle the NDP does not respect property rights, this omission could prove to be very important as the political events of the next few years unfold.

It is often said that there is no need to insert a protection of the right to own and enjoy property in the constitution because the common law already provides adequate protection. If that is the case, why has the NDP insisted that no provision be included in the constitution? If it would make no difference to the protections that are afforded property owners, why not include property rights just for the sake of symmetry?

While elimination of the notwithstanding clause and the extension of the Charter to include the right to own and enjoy property are necessary and would be an excellent start in the direction of improving the constitution, they are not the only changes that could profitably be made. We should seize the opportunity of our current constitutional restructuring to respond to the deep malaise that seems to have infected our polity, not only in Quebec but pervasively. We should also eliminate the reverse discrimination provisions from the Charter.

Stop Fiscal Encroachment: A Tax Limitation Clause

First, we should adopt a constitutional provision that would stop fiscal encroachment by the state. Even if we had property rights in the constitution and eliminated the notwithstanding clause, we would still face the problem of the average citizen losing control over spending power year by year as governments absorb an increasing fraction of the total through increases in the average tax rate. Maintaining a right to property in a constitution which permits the government to encroach on 90 per cent of the country's income is a constitutional oxymoron. For this reason, an increasing number of eminent economists, including Milton Friedman and James Buchanan, have called for a tax limitation clause to be imbedded in constitutions.

Deficit Limitation Clause

Recognizing that taxes can also be deferred from the current crop of taxpayers to a future group via a deficit, there must also be a constitutional provision that no government be permitted to incur tax liabilities beyond its mandate.[7] In effect, this is tantamount to a requirement that every government balance the budget during its term of office, which in turn is a politically adjusted version of the "balance the budget over the economic cycle" requirement that most economists seem to accept.

The Right to Petition for a Constitutional Convention

There are two final requirements that would round out the individual sovereignty approach to constitution making which would speak to the political malaise and provide a check on the power of Parliament which is lacking at the moment. One provision is the right of citizens to petition for a constitutional convention for the purpose of constitutional change. There are a number of good reasons for including this provision, but the main one is that it would act as a discipline on the rent-seeking behaviour which can otherwise dominate the political process. An example of how the ability to petition for a convention can work is to be found in the introduction of a directly elected Senate in the United States. There had been great opposition to the notion by the then appointed (i.e., without election) Senate in spite of widespread support for the idea and the fact that senators from Oregon were already being elected. The Senate did not relent until it looked very much as though a constitutional convention would be successfully initiated. Then the senators pre-empted the constitutional convention so that they could set the terms of the process by which they would be elected.

Referenda and Recall

In dealing with the sense of powerlessness felt by many taxpayers, it may also be instrumental to implement a program of citizen-initiated referenda and provide the possibility for the recall of political representatives who fail to represent the interests of those who have elected them. I do not pretend to have examined the ramifications of these two proposals, but they do seem to offer the possibility of correcting the "dictatorship effect" which characterizes the Canadian political system once elections have been held and a majority parliament is elected. These ideas should at least be explored as possibly beneficial additions to our system of democracy.

Delete the Reverse Discrimination Provisions

Section 15 of the Constitution Act of 1982 provides in subsection 1 that no Canadian will be discriminated against because of race, sex, disability etc. Subsection 2 of the same Section notes that the first Section does not mean that governments may not enact laws that are intended to ameliorate past discrimination. What the subsection implies is that subsection 1 holds unless the government has decided that a reverse discrimination program should be undertaken. If there is such a program, the rights of those who are affected by such programs are simply forfeited in the interest of achieving the aims of the program.

This reverse discrimination or affirmative action provision, in effect, means that there is no protection for individuals from discrimination against them by Parliament if Parliament deems that in some past period of time some group covered by the subsection was discriminated against. At the moment, for example, there is a program of discrimination against young male university teachers. Since this emerges from the intent to hire more female university teachers, males are denied what would otherwise have been the protection of the constitution in seeking redress.

While we should protect the right of private citizens to choose without limit the interactions they will have with their fellow citizens, we should not permit our governments to discriminate between people on the basis of inherent characteristics such as race or sex. The provisions of subsection 2 essentially entitle them to do so, with potential consequences which are spelled out in the Fraser Institute book *Discrimination, Affirmative Action and Equal Opportunity*. Section 15, subsection 2, is a denial of fundamental rights and should be removed.

Notes

[1] The manifestations of some of our political leaders notwithstanding, I am sure that the notion of a divine connection is not currently a practical consideration.

[2] McGregor C. Dawson, *The Government of Canada* (Toronto: University of Toronto Press, 1964), p. 5.

[3] *Ibid.*, p. 75.

[4] The Parti Québécois Government used the notwithstanding clause on a regular basis as the preamble to its legislation, whether the area of the legislation was covered by the provisions of the clause or not.

[5] It was argued by several participants at the McGill University symposium where I first presented this paper that this suggestion is in effect coercion by the back door. According to this view, taxation is coercion and to take money from the whole population of Quebec and use it to encourage English speakers to use French signs is itself a violation of peoples' rights. In answer to this point, it is useful to consider Milton and Rose Friedman's comment in their book *Free to Choose*, to the effect that we must distinguish between a situation where 80 per cent of the population decide to tax 100

per cent of the population in order to subsidize 20 per cent, from one where, via special interest group pressure, 20 per cent of the population contrive to tax the other 80 percent in order to benefit themselves.

In other words, since even those who believe in a limited government agree that there are some purposes for which a super-majority—near unanimity for practical purposes—would agree to levy a tax, and since that same super-majority could pass a constitutional amendment to accomplish the same objective, it seems preferable to use the tax and subsidy route rather than the constitutional route. The reason is that the tax and subsidy route does not involve prohibition of English—clearly a violation of what should be fundamental rights in any constitution.

I should be quick to add that I would not, in general, support the use of tax and subsidy approaches to problems. Later in the paper I argue that the encroachment of the state via the tax mechanism is itself a separate problem which requires attention.

[6] See the entry by Robert Shepherd in the *Canadian Encyclopedia* (Edmonton: Hurtig, 1989), p. 407.

[7] For further discussion of this point see Michael Walker, *Focus on Balancing the Budget* (Vancouver: The Fraser Institute, 1982).

The Individual and the Nation: Natural Allies

Andrew Coyne

A Sense of Nationhood

WE HAVE HEARD SOME SAY that, objectively, everything is fine with Confederation. Canada has achieved one of the highest standards of living in the world. We have one of the freest nations in the world, and one of the highest levels of social development. Certainly there is a compelling logic to this, but I might note that the substance and symbol, objective and subjective, are not so easily separated. A nation state in which large sections of the population doubt its legitimacy, however successful it may be by objective measures, fails on the key test of creating a sense of nationhood.

Importance of Individualism

I want to divide this presentation into two parts. The first will lay out a conceptual framework for thinking about such terms as the individual, the nation and the state. In the second part I will assemble a sort of smorgasbord of constitutional proposals which may be seen to have that conceptual link between them.

The Individual, the Nation and the State

John Fowles, the English writer, said that narcissism consists in this: "When we grow too old to believe in our own uniqueness, we become obsessed with our complexity." [1] What I want to suggest is that what afflicts Canada, as a nation-state, is that the design of its institutions, its practices and policies, and its system of government are essentially narcissistic. Rather than aspiring to universal values reflecting the universal values of human governments, we have instead been acting to preserve our uniqueness and to reflect our complexity. We have been convinced, of course, of our uniqueness, and latterly we have become obsessed with our complexity.

Statism, Groupism and Individual Rights

There are two consequences to this, or two ways in which this is manifest. One is the tradition of statism in Canadian government, not only in the sense of a lack of complete commitment to democratic values, to democratic ways of social choice, but also in the sense of an incomplete commitment to individual rights which is reflected in a rather late and rather emaciated charter. The second is that we have a conviction that group identities, group rights, and group representation are all that matter.

These two fields of statism and groupism are inimical, not only to the individual, but also to the nation, because they weaken individual identity. On the one hand they lead to alienation, to a sense among individual Canadians that they are not really part of anything, and not participating, not fully involved in any larger collective process. On the other hand, they reward fractiousness. Differences which in other nations are resolved through the political arena, however hotly contested they may be, in Canada become threats to the existence of the nation-state; they contribute to a division along regional lines, particularly, and also along ethnic and other lines. Each of these exacerbates the other. Statist economic policies—the practice of handing out regional grants and subsidies, of conferring privileges in the form of monopolies and barriers to entry, and so on—inflame what would otherwise be reasonably benign ethnic and regional differences.

Now these two characteristics, statism and groupism, derive from policy concepts of what a nation is—i.e., the nation both internally and in its relation to other nations or other divisions of humanity—and from how it perceives itself and the individual. The statism part of it comes from a misidentification of the nation in reference to the world at large. In much of the literature on nationalism, there are ways in which people divide nationhood into two camps. The English thinker, Ernest Gellner, spoke of a cultural versus volunteeristic basis of nationality. A German historical critic described them as predetermined or self-determined. Pierre Trudeau distinguished between social and juristic senses. What it amounts to is this: Does the nation exist independently of the will of the people who make it up? Does it simply pre-exist, or is it something the people create themselves through acts of social choice, through their own minds? To put it even more briefly: Is the nation something you are or something you do?

If you accept the first definition, if you say that there is some independent Canadian identity which exists self-evidently, then it quickly becomes the job to enlist the state in one's support if one feels that this identity is being threatened in any way. Indeed, statism in Canada has become part of the Canadian identity. Canada is a nation which puts up tariffs. You saw this during the Free Trade Agreement process. It was simply un-Canadian to take down tariffs. And statism affects a whole measure of other policies. Any time any policy is adopted that might happen to exist in the United States, it is by itself wrong, and not only wrong but un-Canadian and therefore evil.

There is a similarity in this regard between Canadian and Quebec nationalism. As opposed as they may seem to be, they both derive from the sense that identity is what matters and the state should be enlisted to protect that difference, that distinction, that distinctiveness. Now the implication of this model of nationalism is that there's no higher purpose for a nation than its existence. Preserving differences is an end in itself and identity is devoid really of any context—historical or global. You can't have one identity today and a different identity 50 years ago. So what do you do? Well, you obliterate the past and you rewrite history. So we have the idea that Canada has always been essentially a social-democratic state, that the Canadian individual is simply social-democratic man, and that Canada is different and distinctive from other countries in this regard.

Ultimately this is unfulfilling and unsustainable, not only because in many respects we are not that different from the United States, and there are greater differences within the country, but also because Canadians have had a growing awareness that this isn't enough—there has got to be more to a nation than just being different.

Now maybe (just to move on to the other model of nationhood in this respect) we ought to adopt the American model, which is that nationhood has a purpose. Its purpose is indeed in a certain way the state, that is to say to create a system of just laws. Without a social consensus on nationhood, and the idea of nationhood, there is no basis for creating a system of just laws. It follows that the state does not create the nation but the nation in a sense creates the state. The state only defines the nation insofar as you can say that the nation is that which is engaged in creating the state. It is in other words a self-governing people. And the purpose of that state is to reflect the highest human values which we have increasingly come to realize worldwide are universal human values: liberty, democracy, and, I would argue, a market economy—in short, individualistic models of government social choice.

The market is misunderstood, not only by its critics but also by its supporters, as being essentially individualistic, anarchic, and so on. I'd argue that the market is essentially a communitarian device and that its benefit is that it integrates individual wills into a socially beneficial order. Far from chaos, it is a spontaneous order that is brought about and much preferred to the jungle of interest-group politics, and it is *order* because it is based on individual will, on choice, on volunteerism. There can be no black market, for example, in a free market economy.

The other characteristic that I spoke about was groupism. Again this involves two conceptions of the nation, and we've chosen the wrong one in Canada. One conception of the nation, as I've been implying, sees it as a neuro-network of individuals whose participation in these acts of social choice becomes knitted together. The other sees it as essentially a jigsaw puzzle of groups. The job of our constitution, and our system of government as well, is somehow to hold these groups together as best we can and to make the nation up in that kind of jigsaw puzzle way.

What I want to argue, in contradiction to the latter view of the nation, is that ultimately the individual and humanity at large (the two ends of the spectrum) are the only real valid units of humanity, and only valid because they are the only ones which exist independently of those who make them up. The group, the nation, are simply states of mind. They only exist because we decide they will, but individuals and humanity exist independently of that. Moreover, whatever differences there may be between groups are infinitesimal compared to their filial likeness in the family of man, and whatever similarities there are between members of the group that identify them as a group are infinitesimal, again in comparison to their differences as unique individuals. Yet to read our public debates in the newspapers each day, one would think that the only unit that counts is the group, the ethnic group, the national group, the regional group, or what-have-you.

When you find statism and groupism combined, you get that kind of narrow grasping nationalism by which we have been so long afflicted in Canada. I think there's a more positive nationalism, which sees the nation as basically a staging point on the continuum between the individual and humanity. But the nation and the nation state have validity and purpose only so far as they support the welfare of the individual and allow the individual to contribute to human endeavour. That means we should be directing our energies toward the universal—not toward our uniqueness and complexity, but towards universal human values. In constitutional terms this gives purpose to our existence as a nation. It should be our explicit intent to write a constitution which could with minor modifications be adopted by any country on earth.

Some Constitutional Proposals

Guiseppe Mazzini,[2] the Italian nationalist, said that every nation has the right to consider a mission to fulfill for mankind. Equating universal and individual values, as I have mentioned, demands that the nation only has liberty to act when it leads the individual to wider regions and, similarly, to act towards groups within the nation insofar as they do not interfere with the individual and the nation.

As I noted in the title of this paper, the nation and the individual are in this sense allies. By strengthening the individual and by creating this connection, unmediated by provincial interlopers, between the individual and the nation, we can strengthen the individual, the nation and the community at large. One model of that, of course, is the Charter, and it was pretty much the explicit intent of the charter to forge this link in peoples' minds between the individual and the nation. But I think we should go much further, so let me suggest that we must, as our over-arching intent, plug the individual in at every point in the matrix of social choice.

First, and in broadest terms, we should abandon all attempts at state promotion of something called the Canadian identity, be that cultural, economic, or political.

Second, we should be moving towards open borders in Canada. As long as we are intent on keeping the border as a barrier because whatever is outside will somehow be a threat to our identity, be it broadcasts, imports of goods and services, or people, then we're still locking to the identity mind-set and all the weaknesses that entails.

Third, we should be moving toward a much strengthened Charter, abandoning not only the notwithstanding clause, but also restricting its scope.

Fourth, some form of economic constitution could limit the discretionary powers of the federal state. It would also inhibit the provincial power to interfere in market processes (e.g., correcting for externalities, public goods, etc.) without negotiation, thus preventing rent-seeking and therefore the fractiousness between groups that always ensues.

Fifth, I would move to proportionate representation in the Commons, because proportionate representation leads to a broader spectrum of parties and allows the individual a clearer doctrinal difference between the parties to chose from. What we have had in Canada, through elite consensus, is an elite combination model—an ideological sterilization of Canada politics through partisan identification.

I think we should make much more use of referenda in Canadian politics on major issues. The people are the chief executive; they may chose, as any chief executive does, to delegate certain tasks on a day-to-day basis, but if they choose to make major decisions themselves, that is their prerogative. I would also move to much more democratically based federal institutions, including an elected Bank of Canada board, and an elected Supreme Court.

Further, I think we have to devolve a much more mass-participatory form of capitalism. One of the greatest social divides in our country is not between men and women, French and English, or black and white, but between those who own capital and those who do not. In a nominally capitalist society, we continue to have only about 20 per cent of adults owning shares in corporations.

There are two particular veins I would pursue on this. One would be a mass distribution of shares in corporations, as is now being evolved in Eastern Europe. We might follow them with our own form of *perestroika*. The second would be a national stock savings plan which, simply by virtue of its broader opportunities for investment (not only in corporations of a particular province but across the country) would essentially put the provincial stock savings plans out of business.

Last but most important is the constitutional convention, an elected body of delegates who will meet for the one purpose and the one occasion of redrafting the constitution. Results will then be put to a referendum because it is only by such a blockbuster of legitimacy that we can shove the premiers off the stage, that we can destroy once and for all the contract theory of confederation, and, as Pierre Trudeau has argued, establish the notion of "people sovereignty" in this country.

Notes

[1] John Fowles, *Daniel Martin* (Boston: Little Brown and Company, 1977), p. 13.

[2] Guiseppe Mazzini, *The Living Thoughts of Mazzini*, ed. Ignazio Silone (New York: Longmans Green and Co., 1939). p 120.

Section II

The Meech Lake Debacle

Executive Federalism and the Lessons of Meech Lake

Andrew Cohen

Negotiating Meech Lake

AS WE GATHER TO EXAMINE the future of federalism and Canada, I am reminded of events in Ottawa on the evening of June 2, 1990. The premiers and the Prime Minister gathered to make one last effort to save the Meech Lake Accord and, for some, to save the country itself. When the first ministers entered the Museum of Civilization in Hull and took their places at the dinner table on the top floor, the sun was setting across the river, bathing the Parliament Buildings and the Supreme Court in shades of gold and rust. It was an evocative, romantic scene, no doubt to remind the first ministers of the urgency of their deliberations. With a touch of black humour, one of them said, "The road to Hull is paved with good intentions."[1]

As it turned out, it would be a dinner of many courses which would last several days. The nation builders would emerge after a week of exhausting negotiations to declare the renewal of Canada, as they had twice before in the short, unhappy life of the Meech Lake Accord. Of course, this renewal was nothing of the sort. Their agreement would collapse in acrimony about two weeks later. However, they buried more than a clutch of constitutional amendments that night. In their failure to save the Accord, they also failed to save themselves, their power and position, and their traditional role in writing the country's constitution. With the Accord went the process which had produced it. And for the premiers, battered and broken as they were, the greatest insult was that few Canadians seemed to care very much.

Executive Federalism in Disarray

A year later, executive federalism is in disfavour in Canada, and so are the premiers—those, that is, who remain in office. In the talk of re-inventing Canada, no one talks of re-inventing the premiers. For the purposes of nation building, if they did not exist we would not invent them. In fact, if there is a theme in the deluge of recent proposals on constitutional change, it is a deep, visceral desire to circumvent the first ministers and to transfer power from the politicians to the people. A national referendum, a constituent assembly, a dedicated election, a citizen's forum—all reflect a desire to remove this responsibility from the purview of the premiers and the prime minister.

For 25 years, we should remember, it was through the first ministers that Canada tried to change its constitution. The practice had taken root in the 1960s, and by the 1980s, it had become virtually a fourth branch of government, both creating Meech Lake and benefiting from it. Richard Simeon of Queen's University calls Meech Lake, in intent, "a textbook example of executive federalism." While Pierre Trudeau had always been reluctant to convene the premiers to talk about anything, particularly the constitution, Brian Mulroney enjoyed their company. With his commitment to cooperative federalism, the provinces became more powerful and the premiers, as their representatives, more prominent. The premiers were national decision makers and national celebrities. With federal/provincial conferences now on national television, each premier could look forward to a few minutes to pronounce on grain subsidies or stumpage fees. Afterwards they would elaborate to the assembled media hungry for the musings, as the late Eugene Forsey put it, of the "Portentous Vander Zalm" and "The August Devine."

Nonetheless, they did have power and were becoming more powerful. The central government was willing to cede authority, as it had to Newfoundland over offshore resources, or to reduce its fiscal presence because of its deficit. In this age of austerity, the federal portion of provincial revenues was shrinking and the provinces were spending more in those shared areas of jurisdiction. With their majority governments, the premiers could command the loyalties of their cabinet, their caucus and their legislatures. Hence, the deals they made and the agreements they signed with the prime minister could, and did, become the law of the land. Administrative agreements between levels of government were proliferating. In the absence of a body representing the provinces at the centre, the premiers could claim to speak for their regions. It was an authority their predecessors could not have imagined, and it was growing all the time. Cooperative federalism was now co-optive federalism.

It should be said that while executive federalism had become a vehicle for constitutional reform, this did not guarantee its success. In fact, for much of the last half century, executive federalism was something of a failure. As Alan Cairns of the University of British Columbia points out, Canada had not enjoyed a "golden age of executive federalism in constitutional matters" before Meech Lake. The premiers had in fact failed many times to implement constitutional change, and the federal government had acted unilaterally. Even the 1981 agreement cannot really be called a success for executive federalism because it was largely shaped in public and driven by the people. In truth, it is in the workings of administrative cooperative agreements between the provinces and the federal government that executive federalism was most effective.

At Meech Lake, though, the premiers sought to enhance their authority as nation builders. They all won a veto on changes to federal institutions which meant that they could, for example, exclude the creation of new provinces so as not to dilute their power. (It was bad enough to be one-tenth of the power-wielding elite; they would never countenance being one-eleventh). They could prevent the reform of the Senate, so as not to be dislodged as regional representatives. They could nominate Supreme Court judges and senators, a power more real than apparent because authority lay more with the nominator than the selector. More pointedly, they managed to entrench in the constitution annual meetings on the economy and constitutional reform, in perpetuity. There would be meetings whether there was something to discuss or not. Hence, executive federalism would be carved in stone. This provision was the ultimate triumph of the premiers, the logical extension of their vainglory and vanity. There was some poetic justice that it died with the Accord.

If Meech Lake was a textbook example of changing the constitution through executive federalism, it was a colossal failure. A year later, one asks why the first ministers failed and what it says about the process they chose.

The Lessons

There are many lessons to draw from Meech Lake, but one of the most important is the emptiness of executive federalism. The accord showed that executive federalism, in the form of federal/provincial meetings, is an anachronistic instrument of constitutional change in the 1990s. In a pluralistic and egalitarian society, it smacks of exclusivity. Elite accommodation is no longer acceptable in Canada as a form of making constitutions. The importance of this cannot be overstated.

From the beginning of the talks which produced the Meech Lake Accord, the first ministers ensured that Canadians were told as little as possible. The argument that Quebec's proposals were nothing new—that these changes had all been offered before—was a thinly-disguised rationalization for negotiating behind closed doors. In reality, there was no public consultation until after the fact, and even then there were few public hearings. That approach might have been fine in another era. Brian Mulroney talked as if constitutions could still be made the way the Fathers of Confederation had done it—in private, in profanity, plied with liquor. Consider his comments in the spring of 1990:

> In Charlottetown, the boys arrived in a ship—and spent a lot of other time in places other than the library. This is the way it was done. This is the way Confederation came about. There was no great public debate and there were no great public hearings. It became a kind of tradition.

It was a tradition he no doubt wanted to perpetuate. Mulroney, the purveyor of favour and the merchant of persuasion, seemed to enjoy this negotiation by exhaustion.

But what the first ministers learned from Meech Lake before it failed is that although Canadians may not be passionate about the constitution, although they may not stay up all night debating the notwithstanding clause or pondering the meaning of the distinct society, they resent having one imposed on them. They affirmed that the constitution was the property of the people, not of politicians. This was the legacy of 1981 and the Charter of Rights and Freedoms. It served to empower Canadians and to enfranchise them. The Charter had been shaped in a carnival of participatory democracy, and the premiers were badly misguided in thinking that they could get away with less consultation this time.

In a sense, Meech Lake was a revolution from above, a regime contrived of politicians, by politicians, for politicians. It was constitution making by stealth. Of course, the secrecy could be blamed in part on the need for unanimity, an argument the so-called revisionists have made in the last year. The trouble is that an informed electorate expects more today.

The premiers denied that impulse to openness. They denied that constitutions must be made differently. Meech Lake was chosen as the site of the first meeting in order to avoid, as one advisor put it, "having every bloody interest group outside the door." That obsession with secrecy created problems later on. It undermined public faith in the process and created particular problems for Quebec. When, in the three years after Meech Lake, Bourassa claimed that he could not compromise because he already had—that his five conditions were a minimum—he was not dissembling. Quebec had compromised. But it had made its concessions in private and received no political credit for them.

The premiers never seemed to understand the need for public consultation, and tried hard to avoid it. They did indeed meet in secret, not once, not twice, but three times. Not once did they have an open session. In 1987, after they had hatched the deal, five of them refused even to hold public hearings in their legislatures. When the others did, it was with the *caveat* that nothing could be changed lest the whole deal unravel. It was a take-it-or-lose-it proposition.

It was galling to hear Joe Ghiz of Prince Edward Island, at the final session on that Saturday night in Ottawa—a day that will be known as the premiers' last stand, their Battle of Little Big Horn. Ghiz, in his concluding remarks, slammed the process but exonerated the first ministers. "We didn't invent it, we inherited it," he said of the need for unanimity. Well, as Grant Devine, that other great sage of Saskatchewan, once said, you could get away with saying anything on television. You can even persuade people to believe that the amending formula of 1982 forced the premiers to write a constitution in three private, marathon sessions, with no public participation.

Meech Lake showed that you could not operate this way—you could not deny the people their say. If proof were needed it could be seen both during the debate over Meech Lake and now after it, in the process of reconstituting Canada which has taken place in the past year.

During the debate the first ministers, confident they had the support of Parliament and the provinces, were initially prepared to ignore the views of major interest groups, and finally public opinion itself. In the absence of parliamentary opposition—all the provinces and all three parties were for the Accord—it was those interest groups which marshalled public opinion. Northerners, women, aboriginal people, multicultural groups, francophones outside Quebec and anglophones within it had reasons to dislike the Accord. They helped sow doubts. Over the three years, public opposition to the Accord grew. Indeed, it could probably be said that the more Canadians knew about the Accord, the more they doubted the claims of its architects. With the exception of Clyde Wells, Gary Filmon and Frank McKenna, the premiers were prepared to ignore that scepticism. And that's why people were so angry afterwards. Not only were they not consulted, but when they did register their opinion, no one listened.

Their anger found expression afterwards. It is no surprise that the first government to go to the polls after the Meech Lake Accord died was defeated. That David Peterson should go down in Ontario, after five years of remarkable public support which never went below 42 per cent, was a reflection of raw anger. The same anger is likely to defeat the Social Credit Party in British Columbia and the Conservatives in Saskatchewan later this year [they did—Eds.]. Although Meech Lake alone cannot explain why seven of the premiers who signed the accord are no longer around—Peterson, Richard Hatfield, Howard Pawley, Brian Peckford, John Buchanan, William Vander Zalm and Grant Devine—it is a strong reason for the general disenchantment with politicians in the 1990s. That dissatisfaction over Meech Lake and executive federalism also explains the splintering of the party system and the realignment of Canadian politics, which could produce five parties in Parliament next time, none with more than sixty seats.

To measure the depth of the distaste for executive federalism, consider what has happened since Meech Lake. Suddenly, the federal government has discovered participatory democracy. Brian Mulroney is going to consult the country to death and freely says so. Never again will he talk about rolling the dice, the metaphor for manipulation and one-upmanship represented by Meech Lake. By the time the government is finished, there will not be a living, breathing Canadian who has not had his or her say, if he or she wants it. The government has not only established the Citizen's Forum, but two parliamentary committees. Most of the provinces have their own committees. Quebec, for its part, has had two. What this means is that the government wants to allow Canadians their say. Even if it does not listen to them, it can at least offer the appearance of public consultation.

What they are hearing, these tribunes of the people, are a number of proposals to let the country speak. The most popular is the constituent assembly. Another is a national referendum. Both are means to circumvent the premiers, to avoid another gathering of eleven men—all white, Christian, affluent, middle-aged—in a lodge by a lake. It is to prevent them from dictating the words of a national constitution and handing them to the grateful masses on stone tablets. Of course, at some point, provincial ratification will be necessary. But the groundwork will be done in public, and the premiers circumvented.

A New Constitution

In substance, as well as process, the new constitution is likely to limit the role of the premiers. It is also likely to take aim at executive federalism. While the provinces may indeed win more powers, the premiers are likely to have fewer. An elected, equal and effective Senate in Ottawa will strengthen regional representation at the expense of the premiers. The provinces will now express their grievances at the centre, through elected representatives, rather than through the premiers.

The Meech Lake Accord may have set in train events which will enrich the provinces, but not necessarily their premiers, and certainly not in a role as nation builders. Meech Lake was the last of the Constitutional Wars in which the premiers will be captains. The next time they will be casualties. From now on, making constitutions in Canada will be far different. Old premiers may never die, but as nation builders they will fade away. The country will be better off for it. Happily, without a tear, Canada will bid them *adieu*.

Notes

[1] Quotations in this essay are taken from interviews conducted by the author for his book, *A Deal Undone* (Toronto: University of Toronto Press, 1991).

Flaws of the Meech Lake Accord

Eric Maldoff

Shortfalls and Errors

MY TASK IS TO ADDRESS some of what we should perhaps have observed coming out of the last constitutional round of the Meech Lake process, and also perhaps provide some sense of the "lay of the land" in Quebec. I'd like to go right into an examination of the shortfalls that might be observed out of the Meech Lake round, because if we are going to have any success in a new round it is absolutely essential that we learn some lessons from a conference that was dismally unsuccessful. There were a number of errors, and while I don't intend to discuss all of them, there are a few that really warrant highlighting.

The Canadian Character

I might start by saying that I think that among the provincial premiers and the Prime Minister there was an astonishing lack of understanding of the Canadian character. This is a very simple statement I am making, not some sort of highly sophisticated "What is the character of the nation?" statement. Essentially, eleven men went away on a retreat to Meech Lake. Yes, Quebec had put its constitutional demands on the table some time before that meeting, but it was essentially billed as a first ministers' meeting, and our first ministers do get together from to time to time. It was not billed as the critical moment when a constitution would be written for the country. In the period leading up to the great announcement of an agreement of the eleven first ministers in April 1987, no public process had gone on. There had been no hearings, there had been no debate, there had been no discussion, there had been no invitation to the public. Certainly, people in intellectual and political circles were aware of what Quebec wanted; people had attended the Mont Gabriel conference where the Minister of Intergovernmental Affairs of Quebec announced his position, and in the so-called constitution-making industry there was a buzz about this. But if you were a normal citizen of Edmonton, Moose Jaw, or even Quebec, you would not have felt that you were in the midst of a constitutional process. Suddenly, the eleven first ministers emerged from the room and announced they had reached unanimous agreement.

Whatever the merits of the Meech Lake achievement, some in this country heralded unanimity as an achievement in itself. The fact of the matter is that the first ministers came out feeling that their unanimity was of historic moment. They told the Canadian people straight out: This is not discussable, this is not negotiable, this is a seamless web, a perfect document, and if you don't think it is perfect, well then, we can't always have perfection. But whatever you think of it, keep it to yourself, because this is going through.

There was no agreement on hearings in any particular location and no province committed itself to any public process. In fact, throughout the process, many provinces never did hold hearings on the Meech Lake Accord. Drawing from my own experience of travelling across this country, I have never been able to tell a fellow Canadian, whether in Quebec or elsewhere, "This is it, take it or leave it" without them taking a swing at me. There is something of that in our character, in spite of the fact that many allege we don't have an identity. One of the elements of our character is we don't quite agree with that way of proceeding. It's just a matter of principle, of the way we function—we don't like politicians bossing us around that way, and therefore our reaction to Meech Lake was not surprising. I was just surprised at how little understanding of the people and their mentality was reflected in the participants thinking they could play out such an important process in that way.

Ignoring the Charter

The second failure that I would mention is, I dare say, a fundamental failure to understand the 1982 Constitution Act. The new constitution of Canada produced a very significant and real change in the political psychology of this country. Essentially, up to 1982 the constitution of Canada was the domain of governments. It involved negotiations between governments about their prerogatives, their powers, questions of the rights of citizens, and jurisdictional debates as to whether the federal government or individual provinces had the jurisdiction to pass the legislation in question. The constitution of 1982 entrenched a Charter—a Charter flawed by the notwithstanding clause which allows rights to be overridden by legislative majorities—and the effect of that Charter, I think, was to make individual Canadians feel an ownership stake in the Constitution. Maybe Canadians never articulated that feeling, but I think they took it quite seriously. They felt secure in having a Charter, there was pride in the Charter, and there was wide and massive support for the Charter even in Quebec, in spite of the fact that the government of Quebec refused to sign.

Role of the People

That public phenomenon seems to have been completely overlooked in the Meech Lake process. Governments thought they could get together to make a deal about the prerogatives of government, and the people would be told and would assent to it. There even seemed to be a disregard for the fact that under the 1982 constitution the provincial legislatures had a role in constitutional amendment. Just because premiers happened to agree, and the Prime Minister happened to agree, did not ensure constitutional amendment. The constitution itself spells out that the requisite approval is from the legislature, the elected body. And in that context, one would know if elections were imminent in certain provinces. Consequently, the idea of embarking on a process which did not engage the people and attempt to develop consensus was a strategic error, if nothing else, of major proportions. But I think that one of the lessons learned is that that kind of executive federalism is probably dead and buried. I doubt that there are any first ministers who would suggest that approach again.

Partisanship

In addition to the fact that Meech Lake showed utter disregard for the need for consensus, and to the mistaken belief that it was a proper government action, a third error was that partisanship played an enormous role in the Meech Lake process. I would suggest (and I may be disclosing my bias) that one of the strong motivations of the Meech Lake process was an interest on the part of the federal government in securing an electoral base in Quebec.

That approach closed a lot of doors. Once there was a deal, attempting to find a way to deal with the concerns of citizens became far too important. The federal government had decided that it would stand shoulder to shoulder with Quebec and be perceived as the defender of Quebec; it got to the point where the government of Quebec never even had to reject a proposal because the federal government was prepared to do so for it. There are numerous other elements of partisanship that entered into the Accord, but there was no bi-partisan effort to really bring people together on the process. I think it must be acknowledged that constitutional reform, given its enduring nature, must be the type of reform that can stand the test of time—and certainly the test of three years to ratification.

Flaws in Content

The fourth error of the Meech Lake Accord lay in substantial flaws in content. In the government's rush to secure a Quebec base, Quebec was offered goodies that went beyond even what it had requested. For example, one of Quebec's five initial requests was that it be recognized as a distinct society in the preamble of the constitution. It was explicit policy of the Liberal Party of Quebec at the time that the federal government at Meech Lake offer spontaneously to turn the distinct society motion into an interpretive clause, and that the entire constitution of Canada be interpreted in light of Quebec being a distinct society.

Furthermore, it suggested a defined role for the government, in the constitution, to promote that distinct society. We can question the merits of that, but what it did among other things was to raise the spectre of the Charter, which the citizens of this country deemed of considerable importance, being interpreted in light of the government's political considerations rather than the balancing of entrenched rights. It raised the spectre of special powers for Quebec, which has always been an enormously contentious issue, but it never dealt with the issue head-on, so the spectre kept hanging out there.

In the rush to reach the Accord one of the *quid pro quos* was an agreement that would have made all institutional reform in Canada subject to unanimous consent of all the provinces and the federal government. This came at a time when western Canada was already pressing for institutional reform. So a reaction in western Canada began to emerge. Westerners reasoned that by trying to cut this Quebec deal to get Quebec's signature on the constitution, a zero-sum game ensured that the West was losing as Quebec was gaining.

I would suggest that these are flaws in content of considerable import. And at the same time, I think there was also a strategic error in attempting to create the notion of a crisis, something we had witnessed before during the Free Trade debate in Canada. This was essentially the government going and cutting a deal, letting the deadline emerge, and then creating a sense of "you either take the deal as it is, or we have the Abyss." That was the strategy that the government employed (i.e., it was not an accident), and this strategy ran directly counter to what I think most would expect in constitutional negotiation. At the same time one cannot discount the fact that in the middle of the ratification period following Meech Lake, the Quebec government decided to run over the Charter, as interpreted by the Supreme Court, and rule that certain provisions of the Bill 178 language law would still apply. That created even more concern in English Canada.

Conclusion

The Meech Lake deal dwelt mostly on past grievances and little on the future, and essentially was cut as a Quebec deal, not a deal in the interest of all of Canada. Those errors absolutely must be avoided in the future.

One of the myths that seems to be emerging in this round is the notion of panaceas and quick-fix solutions. There is a currency in ideas such as a loose confederation and massive decentralization. This is not something that Canadians are seeking. As a matter of fact, in the West and the East of Canada they are seeking more influence at the federal level, not less. And some people are suggesting that we should get rid of multiculturalism and bilingualism, because they work against Canadian identity. I think that shows a fundamental misunderstanding of what Canadian identity is because tolerance, generosity, and our linguistic and cultural diversity are inherent in our culture.

Section III

The Economics of Decentralization

Political Power and Competition

André Raynauld

T HIS PAPER IS DIVIDED INTO two main sections. I will look first at the relationships and interactions between political power and the economic order. Then, in the second section, I will develop a case in favour of a substantial decentralization of powers in Canada that could become an attractive option in tomorrow's circumstances.

Politics and the Economy

The respective roles of political and economic institutions should be a central issue in the present debate on Canada's future. The position of the Parti Québécois as well as the Bélanger-Campeau Commission in Quebec is contradictory and inconsistent on this subject because the underlying reasoning has never been spelled out.

It might go without saying that those in favour of Quebec's independence attach the most importance to political power. By definition, they want all the political levers and instruments because they feel it is the only way to better serve the basic interests of the population and, as they are fond of saying, to assert their identity. The logic of this position is that the more political powers you have, the more economic progress you achieve.

This thesis has no foundation. The historical record shows that economic performance is associated with less government intervention, not more. One has to relinquish political power to improve economic conditions. I am not thinking mainly in terms of internal policy which may be more or less liberal, more or less interventionist. I am referring to explicit transfers of political decision making involved in international treaties such as the Free Trade Agreement with the United States. Still more to the point is the outstanding example of the construction of Europe, which implies a very significant reduction in national political power; presumably this has been accepted in return for economic benefits (although there were other larger considerations involved such as peace and security).

All political systems of government imply by definition a reduction in political power for the constituent entities as compared with full independence. There again, the fundamental reason why countries or communities agree to abandon part of their sovereignty is that there are substantial economic benefits to be gained from participation in larger political units. The truth is that the well-being of a population is associated not with more but with less political power.

At the same time as the sovereigntists extol the virtues of self-government, they argue the opposite: that the nature and location of political power have no impact whatsoever on economic conditions. They argue that Quebec, for example, could take upon itself all political decisions and still derive the same benefits—if not more—from the Canadian economic union. In other words, because political power is so unimportant, the central government could be abolished without changing anything in the economy. Indeed, this is exactly what I heard recently: "Quebec is an open society, we all believe in free trade and we want to maintain the present economic arrangement with the rest of Canada. Therefore, if Quebec achieves its independence, nothing will be changed in the way the economy will be run, and there is nothing to lose." This is a very popular line in Quebec.

In practice, this argument requires that through direct negotiations between themselves, the provinces could achieve the same like-mindedness and set the same common rules affecting all economic agents and institutions as would a federal law on competition or transportation or income tax. Beyond the fact that such unanimity appears as a sheer utopia, especially in a context requiring that the provinces refrain from using their powers to protect their short-term interests, one cannot refrain from asking why Quebeckers want independence if there is nothing to be changed and therefore nothing to be gained in the process.

At this point, one may be forgiven if one thinks that of the two opposite theses presented, it is the first one that is irrelevant. My own conclusions are: first, that there is a clear need for a central government to attend to the tasks that extend beyond the reach of the provinces; and second, that the reduction in political power that this implies may be very beneficial for the well-being of everyone concerned.

There is another debate involving the interaction between government and market forces, and between governments themselves, particularly in federal systems. There will be nothing new in my saying that market forces constrain governments by giving alternatives to economic agents through the mobility of capital and labour and the free circulation of goods and services. Governments are also limited and sometimes neutralized by the reactions of consumers and producers to their decisions. Artificial price policies will move resources in unwanted directions. In his study for the Bélanger-Campeau Commission, Jean-Luc Migué gives pages of examples of inefficient policies leading to disastrous results.[1] However, the fact that those policies are not withdrawn in spite of their being ineffective and harmful is strong evidence that governments can resist. Stated in a positive way, governments still have a major role to play in the establishment and development of market mechanisms.

If internal market forces set limits to government intervention and regulation, the internationalization of activities, trade liberalization and global interdependence will add considerable additional constraints. If governments reduce competitiveness by imposing extra costs of production, the negative impact will be felt sooner, and will be more widespread and damaging than previously. One could go further and say that the population will no longer accept being left behind because people know what goes on in the world.

In this case as in the previous one, however, it is better for all if governments commit themselves to opening their economies on a long-term basis through international treaties such as those negotiated under GATT, the OECD, the Bern Union or regional free-trade zones, rather than relying on *ad hoc* policies which can be reversed at any time.

World trade liberalization and the Free Trade Agreement with the United States have been used in Quebec as an argument in support of separation as an alternative to the Canadian union. This recalls the very old debate on the natural character of North-South trade and the artificial character of East-West trade. Trade statistics are used to show that the importance of interprovincial trade has diminished relative to foreign trade as a consequence of the Kennedy and Tokyo Rounds. Another argument is that Quebec could peg its currency to the U.S. dollar as an alternative to the Canadian monetary union.

There are three answers to these arguments. First, interprovincial trade is still significantly more important for Quebec than foreign trade. Second, a free trade area provides much less economic benefit than an economic union such as the Canadian one. And third, it would be much more advantageous for Quebec, and for that matter for all provinces, to increase their trade both ways—North-South and East-West—rather than play one against the other.

There is an additional very large issue regarding the interaction between government and the economy that has direct reference to federalism. I refer to the very well-known theory that competition between governments is inherent in a federal system and that this competition is what makes federalism a superior form of government.

I do not dispute the fact that there is intergovernmental competition. However, one should not confuse market competition and government competition. Genuine competition leads to efficiency because exchanges are voluntary, prices are freely determined, and there is freedom of choice at little or no cost to consumers. Government competition is a caricature by comparison. Transactions are prescribed or imposed whether consumers like it or not, and resources are levied at the expense of taxpayers. This competition leads inevitably to higher, not lower prices; it is the main reason for duplication of services because services buy votes.

To solve this problem of spurious competition, I would favour a tighter division of powers between the provinces and the central government, and a formal commitment to stick to their own fields of jurisdiction. The substitute for competition is nothing less than the rule of law, in the same way as are the international treaties and undertakings mentioned before in the context of the global economy. This approach would require a radical shift in political philosophy in this country, since all governments want to be all things to all people.

This conclusion on the division of power provides me with a smooth transition to address the issue of constitutional and political reform in this country. I will examine first the general rules which explain and dictate the division of powers in a federal system of government. This will be followed by specific applications amounting to a package of suggested reforms.

Elements of Constitutional and Political Reform

The case for decentralizing government functions rests essentially on the assumption that consumer preferences are different among various groups or communities when it comes to the provision of public goods. Otherwise there would be no justification for the federal system in the first place. And this is true of all federal systems anywhere. Given these differences in consumer demand, it is more efficient, and it is welfare enhancing, to let lower-level governments provide the public goods in differing ways, differing combinations, and with a differing content so as to insure that preferences will be best satisfied.

This proposition is well-established in the literature. One need only refer to Wallace Oates' decentralization theorem which states that, other things being equal, there are efficiency gains in decentralization if preferences are different; the more diversified the preferences, the higher the gains.[2] The same reasoning justifies the concept of subsidiarity in the European Commission: the supra-national authority should only be assigned the functions that cannot be performed efficiently at the lower levels of government.

The gains from decentralization have been identified by Breton and Scott.[3] First, decentralization gives satisfaction to more people by increasing the probability that anyone can become a member of a majority. Second, because provincial and local governments are closer to their market area, they have a chance to know the situation better and adjust their policies accordingly. It is also less costly for individuals to signal or reveal their preferences if they wish.

There are still other gains. Diversity of approach allows experimentation and innovation, which reduces risks (a local mistake is always better than a national one). Finally, there is a two-fold argument about mobility. By producing more efficient policies, decentralization reduces migration and the costs of mobility. At the same time, through mobility, it provides an escape for those who prefer a different mix of policies in another jurisdiction. There is thus less coercion overall than under a unitary form of government.

Tailoring policies and institutional processes to the needs and preferences of the citizens will call for differences in the nature and actual content of policies. Certainly, it militates against setting national standards and priorities about everything just before a federal election.

That being said, there are constraints and limits bearing on the satisfaction of one's preferences. Even individual freedom is limited by the freedom of others. First, public goods are not all produced at the same cost per capita irrespective of the size of population. Second, government decisions may produce spillover effects in other jurisdictions. It then makes sense to transfer decision making to a higher level of government so as to take such spillovers into account or prevent them. Third, regarding private goods, we all accept that there are very substantial gains in having free access to a larger market, and to pools of resources created through specialization, economies of scale, security of supply and so on.

Therefore, decentralization cannot be the only goal of constitutional reform. Consumer preferences may be different, but they also have to be satisfied and the resources must be available. Incorporating these constraints into the analysis one could say: let us have maximum decentralization—while taking into account spillover effects—compatible with the maintenance of the gains arising from the economic integration of the provinces. This formulation brings us to the essence of federalism: it is a system of government which balances the gains from diversity and fragmentation against the gains from free access to a larger market requiring uniformity or at least a level playing field.

The general rules and principles just presented can be translated into specific guidelines such as the following:
1. Removal of all restrictions to the application of the Charter of Rights and Freedoms.
2. Constitutional guarantee of the four basic economic freedoms: the free flow of people, and the free circulation of goods, capital and services within Canada.
3. Elimination of federal spending power in matters of provincial jurisdiction. The use of this power has probably done more than anything else to undermine the federal nature of the Canadian political system. It has led to ruinous duplication of public services and confusion of roles between governments. It goes against any notion of division of powers, which is supposed to be the essence of federalism.

With the elimination of the federal spending power, I am not sure if there is still room for the establishment of so-called national standards. In case there is, I would want to constrain or limit the application of this notion to what is absolutely necessary to achieve the free circulation of goods, services, capital and people. Admittedly, this condition may justify a considerable number of standards and may be less constraining than it looks. Nevertheless a justification is better than the arbitrariness which characterizes the present situation.

There are other solutions to reconcile the need for decentralization and the need for economic integration and mobility. One would be to encourage intergovernmental negotiations so as to harmonize policies and regulations in fields of provincial jurisdiction. A good example of this approach is the recent interprovincial agreement on trust and savings companies.

Indeed this concertation could be institutionalized or even constitutionalized in the form of a required process for use in, say, fiscal policy.

A second, complementary approach would consist in giving a federal status to the Senate, to a number of crown corporations and central agencies such as the Bank of Canada, and to a number of other matters such as communications, housing, the arts and so on. This could be achieved in several ways. Strictly speaking, to give federal status implies giving formal representation to the provinces on the boards of directors. In some cases one could settle for a little less than that, but these are modalities.

One last general component of constitutional reform is equalization. With an eye to the acceptability of the package, I believe that equalization must remain a key feature of the Canadian fiscal system. And by equalization I mean unconditional grants—with no strings attached and no national standards—so as to allow poorer provinces to provide a minimum level of public goods or services if they so wish. I know that equalization may be criticized as providing wrong incentives—as all redistributive measures do. However, although it may not be fully efficient, equity considerations militate in favour of such a system to provide the resources that are necessary for the actual use of the powers and responsibilities that the provinces have.

Conclusion: Towards a Decentralized Canada

With precautions to maintain and perhaps even reinforce the integration of the Canadian economy, the avenue is wide open for an effective and substantial decentralization of the political system. First, with the elimination of the federal spending power, the field loosely defined as social policy would return to the provinces where it belongs anyway in the present constitution. This includes education and training, income security, health, culture, and housing, to which I would add natural resources. (Federal expenditures devoted to social programs and subsidies of all kinds amount to about 35 per cent of total federal spending.) This would represent a huge transfer of fiscal resources to the provinces without any substantial changes in the constitution itself. However, some particular aspects of the matters mentioned would still require federal presence and central policies. International trade in resource products is an obvious example. Other federal programs should be re-examined and reassessed to see if they are really needed at that level of government in the light of previously mentioned efficiency requirements and significant spillovers across provinces.

At the other end of the spectrum, the federal government would also have sufficient exclusive powers to manage the economy and to deal with national and international issues. The main fields that come to mind are defence, interprovincial and international trade and transportation, monetary and fiscal policy, competition policy, and equalization.

In this restructuring process, one could usefully keep in mind the opting-out approach proposed by Tom Courchene, should some provinces or regions be adamantly opposed to any decentralization. This alternative could become a key to the resolution of our differences and the preservation of our respective distinctivenesses.

Notes

[1] Jean-Luc Migué (1991). *Retour du vrai fédéralisme, institutionalisation de la concurrence entre gouvernements.* Commission Bélanger-Campeau. Volume 4, pp. 681-719.

[2] Wallace Oates, *Fiscal Federalism* (New York: Harcourt Brace Jovanovich, 1972).

[3] Albert Breton and Anthony Scott, *The Design of Federations* (Halifax: I.R.P.P., 1980).

Economics and the Renewal of Federalism: Building with the Basics

D.A.L. Auld

Introduction

THERE IS LACKING IN THE current Canadian debate on federalism a clearly stated set of basic economic principles. While I do not dispute the complexity of the issue, and accepting the premise that economics is only part of the debate, I hope the following approach may prove beneficial. There are, of course, competing models of constitutional federalism and only one is chosen here. It may, however, allow us to explore the economic issues in the proper setting.[1]

Allocative Efficiency

Consider a large geographical area that has a unitary, highly-centralized form of government. There are no boundaries separating local-type jurisdictions, although areas are identified as urban or rural. All services—pure public, quasi-public, and collective consumption—are financed and supplied by the central (only) government.

The government tries to be efficient or cost-minimizing. Based on the realization that scale economies (and diseconomies) are important, services are delivered by regional authorities with funding from the central level after accounting for geography and population density; the funding is the same on a per capita basis for all services across the country. In short, there exists a state monopoly with multiple production/delivery points to minimize costs. Private sector substitutes in some cases such as education may appear but no citizen can opt out of taxation.

Assume now that a group of citizens in a public goods delivery area are dissatisfied with the mix of public goods. In their view, roads are substandard and there are too many hockey arenas, given the interest in other recreational pursuits.[2] These citizens persuade the central government to allow the regional "plant" to modify the mix of their output, subject to a budget constraint. The dawn of federalism begins where local preferences dictate the mix of public goods. Since these local goods have only marginal spillovers (i.e., positive externalities) the central government reduces the central tax rate on citizens in the community, allowing them to establish their own taxes to fund local (no or low spillover) goods. A mechanism is established to hold regional elections to ensure that the mix of output of these local goods reflects democratic principles.[3] Federalism is entrenched.

Research over the past three decades has demonstrated that there are social welfare gains from this sort of federalism, in which the shape and nature of the regional club or government is driven largely by concerns for spillovers and cost-minimizing features.[4] In a democracy, people and capital are free to move; with federalism, there can be a better match between output (supply) of and demand for public goods if localized preferences are acceptable.

What if the spillovers and/or economies of scale are significant? Consider the following extreme case: in a country with 25 regional communities, each community is concerned about possible aggression from another country, but the degree of concern varies across the country. Community A wants more per capita spending on the air force and community B wants more per capita spending on the navy. The central government reduces, on an equal per capita basis, central taxes that represent the defence commitment.

Each regional government must now create its own defence force. Most would agree that the solution is ridiculous. Why? First, the spillovers are significant. If Community B's navy deters aggression on the coast, the inland is protected. Community A's air force will protect other communities as well. In addition, there will be very high costs associated with 25 defence forces compared to one.

This is an extreme case. There is widespread consensus that, in terms of personal individual preferences and costs of delivery of public goods, hockey arenas and tennis courts belong in a relatively small jurisdiction while defence, criminal justice and currency are central government matters. The critical issue is the extent of the spillovers associated with any collective consumption within a given geographical area, and hence the size of the appropriate political jurisdiction.[5]

Standards of Public Services

Allocative or technical efficiency dictates to a significant extent the structure of federalism, but there is another element of federalism that cannot be ignored: the standard of the public service. Welfare criteria could result in the establishment of many sub-central governments, particularly in large, densely populated countries, leading to the definite possibility that the quality or level of service associated with a particular public good will differ from jurisdiction to jurisdiction.

The implication of these criteria for federalism depends very much on how the standards of the good or service are defined. One approach would have all constituent members of a federation agree that each jurisdiction will have a universal system of hospital and medical insurance. The design of that plan would be left up to the citizens of each jurisdiction to decide. Another approach would have all jurisdictions agree to an identical hospital and medical insurance system with no deviations whatsoever. A third option would have the central government use its powers of taxation and transfer payments to fiscally "coerce" each jurisdiction into designing and delivering the common system of health care.

An identical system of health care throughout a country means that there are no surprises when people move from one area to another. Public goods no longer influence geographical location. If this is true for all public goods, we revert to the centralized system. If systems differ across jurisdictions, health care may become a factor in decisions to move. Thus, it is argued, human capital mobility is enhanced through at least some common public services across the country as agents respond to private sector forces. But the lack of differences in public goods may, for others, impede mobility.

Do standards hold a country together? By "coercing" some jurisdictions to adopt a central government-imposed level of service, one may actually be setting region against region or at least federal against provincial politicians. Furthermore, centrally-imposed identical public services that are subsidized through transfers do not encourage healthy competition among jurisdictions with respect to service delivery.

The Redistributive Function

On grounds of allocative efficiency, provincial and local government will emerge and, through their legislative assemblies, resources will be allocated to public goods on the basis of regional preferences. If these elected assemblies are partisan and reflect varying social and economic philosophies, social welfare functions will emerge, reflecting the governing party's view on how wealth should be redistributed in that jurisdiction. It has been argued, however, that to allow provincial governments to enact and be responsible for income redistribution would most affect the poor and weak. The consequences would be an undesirable inflow/outflow of citizens from one region to another and a dynamic instability with respect to tax and expenditure policy.[6]

To deny a redistributive desire at the local or provincial level is to deny the very existence of such an elected government. A social welfare function that contains arguments for a mix of private and public goods will surely contain arguments regarding how the citizens in that jurisdiction are treated by that society in terms of both private and public goods consumption. If the social welfare function is a reflection of individual utility functions that in turn depend on other people's utility, there is no escaping the need to recognize a redistribution function at the provincial or even local level.[7]

The social welfare functions of the federal and provincial governments are not likely to be the same, and to the extent the federal government attempts to change the redistributive direction of a province through central tax and expenditure policies, there will be resentment towards the central government.

As noted earlier, it is important to keep in mind that there are two forms of redistribution. The central government can redistribute personal wealth across the federation by way, for example, of a negative income tax. Alternatively, the central government can redistribute wealth by country-wide taxation and redistribution back to lower-level governments.[8] If the flows back to a local government are in the form of unconditional cash transfers, these may flow back to citizens through reduced taxation or increased public goods and services. Alternatively, the central transfer can be made to a lower government with strings attached: spend the grant on health or social welfare, or there is no grant. This latter form of redistribution is seen at times to be an interference with local preferences and is therefore resented.

Conflict is clearly exacerbated when there are different political philosophies represented at provincial and federal levels. If, for example, the federal government's redistributive direction involves subsidies for medicare and housing for lower income families and the provincial government wishes to introduce a negative income tax, neither jurisdiction is completely free to act on its own because of joint "ownership" in the housing, hospital and income tax areas.[9] The outcome may be long delays in the implementation of any policy, compromises which have only moderate support, expensive programs involving duplicate bureaucracies, and the incorrect assignment of fiscal powers. The result is an accumulation of myriad policy changes and new policies which, when taken together, amount to an environment that is actually anti-federation.[10]

Allocative Efficiency and Redistribution in Constitutional Federalism

What Does it all Mean for Federalism?

Alexis de Tocqueville, in his *Democracy in America* wrote "The federal system was created with the intention of combining the different advantages which result from the magnitude and the littleness of nations."[11] Many years later, the political scientist Kenneth Wheare wrote that federalism was "the method of dividing powers so that general and regional governments are each, within a sphere, co-ordinate and independent."[12]

In these definitions of federalism, the constitution should set out explicitly ways in which the autonomy of the different levels of government is protected. This was attempted in 1867 but World Wars, a depression and interpretation of the residual rights clause transformed autonomous provincial rights into shared federal-provincial responsibilities in several areas.

In addition, the transformation of the role of government in general has impacted federalism. It has been argued that over the last 35 to 40 years

Canada has been transformed from a liberal democracy to a welfare democracy. Under the liberal democratic banner, the state defined what citizens could not do and individuals proceeded to do what was necessary to achieve their own destiny. The welfare democratic state has stronger elements defining what freedoms the state has granted to the individual. Emphasis is more on equality of outcome at the expense of individual decision making.

In the federal-provincial arena, this implies more direction from the centre through fiscal coercion and interference with areas of provincial responsibility through such action as the establishment of parallel institutions. To the extent that provincial governments have also moved to welfare democracy, their specific ideas of what constitutes equality of outcome will not likely coincide with other provinces nor, for that matter, with the central government.

Instead of a division of powers reflecting what the constituent parts of Canada desire, the country is closer to a system of power sharing brought about by fiscal coercion, unsatisfactory intergovernmental agreements, and duplication. The most recent pronouncements by the federal government in response to the debate in Quebec underscore the problem. The federal government claims that it will develop a new constitution that will be acceptable to the provincial governments. That is not in my view what federalism is about and is not what a "renewed federalism" should focus on. Instead, Ottawa should be asking all the provinces to meet without the presence of the federal government, and decide on the kind of federation Canada should be—and then Ottawa should facilitate that desire. Recall Wheare's definition of federalism. With the exception of basic federal powers necessary to make any federation work, all issues should be on the table for the provinces to discuss. Currency, the money supply and related financial matters, human rights, all internal free trade, and a minimum standard of living are some of the central powers that all provinces would agree on to ensure that the collective gains of a federation could be achieved.

Summary and Conclusion

The initiative should come from the provinces, not the central government. A central government that dictates how the federation will work is a recipe for failure. A federation in which the central government facilitates the collective desires of the provinces while guaranteeing their autonomy in a specific range of activities will flourish, each part reinforcing the other. To minimize the conflict over the assignment of economic powers and functions, all parties to the debate must recognize: (1) why the allocative function of government logically requires a degree of decentralization; (2) the existence of social welfare functions at different levels of government; and (3) the need for a few, but key, undiluted federal powers.

Notes

[1] See D.A. Auld, *Contemporary and Historical Dimensions of Canadian Confederation* (Canberra: Centre for Research on Federal Financial Relations, 1979).

[2] The notion that gains in welfare can be extracted through decentralization was originally developed by Charles Tiebout, "A Pure Theory of Local Expenditures," *Journal of Political Economy* (October 1956). A formal model of the decentralized therein can be found in Wallace Oates, *Fiscal Federalism* (New York: Harcourt, Brace, Jovanovich, 1972).

[3] As Tresch points out, "It seems obvious, though, that local jurisdictions will create their own social welfare functions, each one distinct from the national social welfare function." Richard W. Tresch, *Public Finance: A Normative Theory* (Georgetown, Canada: Irwin Dorsey, 1981), p. 574.

[4] J. Buchanan, "An Economic Theory of Clubs," *Economica* (February 1985); M. McGuire, "Group Segregation and Optimal Jurisdictions," *Journal of Political Economy* (Jan./Feb. 1974). The externality component of the regional "club" was first highlighted by Buchanan, and a more general, formal model may be found in McGuire.

[5] For a brief but thorough summary of this aspect, see R. Boadway and D. Wildasin, *Public Sector Economics* (New York: Little Brown, 1984), pp. 501-03. Because of mobility between jurisdictions of capital and labour, there may arise *fiscal externalities* that do not produce an efficient allocation of resources. This is fully explored in Boadway and Wildasin, pp. 511-18.

[6] It is important to distinguish between redistribution from the central government to individuals, regardless of location, using country-wide criteria, and redistribution to *regions* or to individuals based on their *location*. As Stiglitz and Courchene have pointed out, the latter may, in the longer run, reduce total welfare in the country as a whole. Joseph E. Stiglitz, *Economics of the Public Sector* (New York: W. W. Norton, 1986), pp. 554-55;

Thomas Courchene, "Avenues of Adjustment: the Transfer System and Regional Disparities," in *Canadian Confederation at the Crossroads* (Vancouver: The Fraser Institute, 1978).

[7] For an interesting discussion regarding the pattern of redistribution when parties of different political philosophies are in power at different levels of government, see A. Breton and A. Scott, *The Economic Constitution of Federal States* (Toronto: University of Toronto Press, 1978), pp. 114-16; and Tresch, *Public Finance*, pp. 593-96.

[8] D.A. Auld and L. Eden, "Federal Provincial Equalization and the Canadian Constitution," *Government and Planning* (1983), I, for a discussion of how the philosophies of redistribution were enshrined in the Canadian Constitution Act of 1982.

[9] Tresch, *Public Finance*, pp. 592-93. Public goods become part of the redistribution plan and the separation of the allocation and redistribution branch is more difficult. In another context, the interdependence of the two branches arises when public goods with decreasing costs are provided at pareto-optimal prices and the "deficit" must be tax-financed.

[10] For a thoughtful and enlightening essay on this and related topics, see Jean-Luc Migué, "Institutionalizing Competition Between Governments: A Return to True Federalism", Brief to the Bélanger-Campeau Commission, 1991.

[11] Alexis de Tocqueville, *Democracy in America*; Phillips Bradley, ed. (New York: New American Library, 1945), I, pp. 80-84.

[11] Kenneth Wheare, *Federal Government* (London: Oxford University Press, 1964), p. 244, also pointed out that the "federal government... stands for multiplicity in unity. It can provide unity where unity is needed, but it can ensure that there is variety and independence in matters where unity and uniformity is not essential."

Fiscal Federalism and the Constitution

Thomas J. Courchene

Introduction

I WILL BEGIN WITH A set of assertions to introduce an analysis of the manner in which fiscal federalism and constitutional concerns interact. Drawn from my recent work,[1] the following assertions constitute the backdrop to the remainder of this paper.

1. Unless "pushed out" by the Rest of Canada (ROC), Quebec won't exit. Simply put, the economic costs are too high.

2. ROC will not push Quebec out. What this means is that the "bon voyage" movement in ROC will begin to taper off. Although the realization is taking time to sink in, the costs, both political and economic, are too high.

3. As we count down to any 1992 referendum, the game is going to shift quite dramatically from the political/constitutional arena (where the axis is Quebec/ROC) to the economic arena (where the challenge of renewing the federation will engage all provinces and indeed all Canadians).

4. If a cleavage develops, it could well be between have and have-not provinces where Quebec, by virtue of its recent economic performance, is roughly neutral with respect to the federal transfer system and will begin to throw its lot behind the have provinces.

5. If we remake the federation only on political/constitutional grounds and ignore the underlying economic imperatives, the "victory" will be pyrrhic and short-lived.

None of this is to suggest that the outcome of the present constitutional crisis will necessarily preserve the Canadian polity. There are simply too many eventualities between now and 1992.

With this as the overall context, I will address the federal-provincial issues or challenges in what amounts to a set of speculations or assertions.

Social Policy "Railway"

As we integrate North-South, what binds us together as a nation is more and more a social policy and value system "railway" rather than an economic policy railway. This is but another way of saying that increasingly the optimal currency area in the Mundell or trade/transactions sense is North-South, not East-West. The related challenge is how do we Canadians maintain our social policy/value system in the context of North-South integration? Several important implications flow from this observation.

The Tax Transfer System as the Redistributive Instrument

In the good old days it was possible to use economic policy measures to redistribute income East-West and away from the Americans (e.g. tariffs, subsidies, two-price systems for energy). With globalization and the Free Trade Agreement, our ability to use the allocative system as a vehicle for redistribution is severely (and, in my view, appropriately) circumscribed. Subsidies will eventually go. For example, long distance telephone rates will become internationally competitive. In other words, the new National Policy will not only be a version of a social contract but it will also be delivered via the tax transfer system.

The FTA and "Place-Prosperity" Transfers

While globalization occurs the political economy of Canada's East-West transfer system will come under increased scrutiny in the context of North-South integration and the FTA (note that while the FTA enhances North-South commerce, this integration was inevitable in any event). Specifically, Ontario's much-heralded magnanimity in terms of existing regional transfers has, in my view, always contained a healthy dose of "Ontario first." As long as trade flowed largely East-West, with Ontario the principal North-South conduit, the second-round spending impacts of regional transfers typically came to rest somewhere in that province. Under full North-South integration this will alter: increasingly, the second-round impacts will come to rest in North Carolina or California. This will serve to undermine both the political and the economic rationale for regional transfers, especially those that privilege place rather than people (as an important aside, to be elaborated later, I view equalization as part of "people" transfers).

MNCs to TNCs

A final point may be made regarding globalization and the transfer system. Globalization is converting multinationals (MNCs) to transnationals (TNCs). MNCs are organizations that are subject to host country requests or requirements as a condition for entry. TNCs enter on equal terms with domestic companies. Provisions like "national treatment" under the FTA or the single European passport scheduled for 1992 allow TNCs to replace MNCs. One implication of this is that the operation of welfare states everywhere are being reconsidered. A dilemma arises because many, if not most, welfare states are geared to their national production machines. As production becomes increasingly international these welfare states are, in varying degrees in various countries, being set adrift. The challenge becomes: what is the optimal nature of a national social contract (i.e. welfare state) in an integrating or globalizing international economy?

Undermining the Social Policy Railway

Keeping in mind external challenges to the social contract, I now turn to some made-in-Canada challenges. The most problematic and, at the same time, high-profile of these can be phrased as follows: given that the current version of Canada's National Policy is along the lines of a social policy railway, Ottawa in its last two budgets seems to be pulling out the "last spike" in financing this interregional transfer system. The federal-provincial transfer system is now in shambles. Equalization is being driven by the ceiling, which for the current year, means that actual payments are running about one billion dollars beneath (non-ceiling) entitlements.

The story of Established Programs Financing is more dramatic. After Ottawa cut back the growth of EPF in the late 1980s to GNP-minus-2 per cent and later to GNP-minus-3 per cent, the effect of the last two federal budgets has been to freeze EPF in nominal terms through to 1995 (except for population growth, which could add one per cent per year). In terms of the Canada Assistance Plan (CAP), Ottawa has capped federal payments to the three have provinces: the transfers can only grow by five per cent each year. To this trio one might also add the privatization-*cum*-cutbacks in Unemployment Insurance (UI), including a 24 per cent increase in premiums in July 1991.

Canada Assistance Plan

Looked at in somewhat greater detail, the cap on CAP "equalizes" the transfers in question. This may be "politically correct," but it represents a dramatic shift in terms of the original rationale of CAP. What it means is that, as a result of the close to $2 billion increase in welfare payments recently, Ontario will receive a five per cent increase in its existing federal CAP payments instead of the near $1 billion addition under the former regime. Indeed, one can legitimately raise the issue of whether Ontario would have embarked on its recently expanded welfare system if it had realized that Ottawa was about to alter its payment program. And as a recent Supreme Court decision makes clear, since these transfer programs are federal programs, they can be redesigned by Ottawa without notice to suit its own needs and/or preferences.

Established Programs Financing

The implications for EPF are in a sense even more dramatic, but not yet broached. Should the EPF ceiling revert to GNP-3 per cent beyond 1995, the eventual result will be that the tax-point component of EPF exceeds the ceiling so that the cash component falls to zero. For Quebec, this will occur about the mid-1990s and for the remaining provinces sometime early in the next millennium (see the following section for elaboration). When the cash component falls to zero, how will Ottawa assert any influence in terms of national standards (for medicare, for example)? One answer is contained in the 1991 federal budget. Ottawa will implement its own version of the golden rule: it will stop supplying the gold, but it will not stop making the rules.

Disappearing Cash Transfers

More daunting with respect to EPF is the Quebec position *vis-à-vis* the rest of the provinces. Quebec receives 16.5 personal income tax points more than the other provinces. This is offset by the fact that Quebec receives an equivalent amount less in federal cash transfers than do the remaining provinces (all provinces were given this option earlier, and only Quebec took advantage of the offer). Of 16.5 points, 8.5 are allocated to EPF. As noted, this means that in a year or two the value of Quebec's tax points for EPF will exceed the overall ceiling. What will happen then is far from clear. At one extreme, the cash transfer will simply fall to zero and stay there. Quebec will then receive EPF payments which, overall, will exceed the ceiling. How long will it take the other provinces to demand the same treatment as Quebec? At the other extreme, Ottawa can insist that the cash payments become negative, i.e., Ottawa will reduce cash transfers to Quebec from other programs such as equalization. This will surely precipitate a dramatic confrontation since it will be viewed by Quebec as a federal confiscation of its tax points.

To understand what is at stake here, some ballpark numbers are in order. The EPF ceiling, in aggregate, is about $20 billion. Of this, just over $12 billion is in the form of tax point transfers with about $7.5 billion in cash transfers. The value of an equalized personal income tax point is in the order of $900 million; if Ottawa were to give all provinces the 8.5 tax points that Quebec has, the result would be roughly equal to the existing cash transfer. Obviously, this is not going to happen, since it would eventually result in an *increase* in EPF transfers compared to the pre-freeze status quo. Some tax point transfer may be needed, however, to get Ottawa out of this impending dilemma.

A Veritable Transfer State

To this point, it probably appears to the reader that I take a dim view of federal initiatives on the transfer front. The timing is most unfortunate in terms both of the phase of the cycle and the ongoing constitutional crisis. When future scholars look back at the decade of the 1980s, the inappropriateness of the Tories' fiscal (and indeed macro) policies will be strikingly evident. Equally inappropriate is the lack of notice typically associated with federal freezes and cuts. Surely the worst political job in this country is that of a provincial treasurer!

That said, however, something has to give on the transfer front, for Canada is becoming a veritable "transfer state." Equalization has gone well beyond the formal equalization program—it includes UI and now CAP as well as many line departments. Changes were designed to achieve "place-prosperity"; in the event, they privilege neither places nor people. Yet there are those who are arguing for extending the formal equalization program to encompass "needs." Specifically, it is argued that the share of federal funding for CAP should be linked to some indicator like the incidence of unemployment. But this would result in a vicious circle. The high Atlantic unemployment rates are to a substantial degree a result of the transfer system, i.e. they are a result of existing (and incentive-distorted) federal largesse. To throw yet more money at this "problem" is to assume that somehow a normal condition represents a disequilibrium. In reality, our entrenched regional disparities represent a policy-induced equilibrium.

The Canadian Economic Union

Even Ottawa, despite its recent initiatives, has not understood its complicity in this situation. For example, one of the thrusts in the recent Throne Speech is an emphasis on competitiveness; within this, a key element is to enhance the internal economic market (or the Canadian economic union). What Ottawa has in mind here is to strike down high-profile impediments like the provincial beer fiefdoms and provincial purchasing preferences. In my view, however, by far the most severe impediments to the operations of the internal common market are those implicit barriers that distort the optimum distribution of people by distorting not only the incentives to migrate but as well the incentives to acquire human capital.[2] Recognition that these implicit barriers serve to fragment the Canadian economic union has not yet infiltrated Ottawa's thinking.

Centralization/Decentralization

Can a fragmented union work? Many Canadians, or at least many non-Quebec Canadians, believe that Canada is already very decentralized—probably too decentralized. There are plenty of comparative "ratios" from other federations and trends within Canada that can ostensibly support such a claim. My view is that Canada can hardly be called decentralized in an effective sense when, in one fell swoop, Ottawa can undermine the fiscal positions of all the provinces. And the worst of the provincial fiscal crunch is probably yet to come.

A second and related observation is that we *will* finally begin to see some effective decentralization. Provinces have the choice of raising taxes to place their existing social programs on a sustainable basis, of altering these "national" programs, or most likely some combination of the two. Either option will enhance effective decentralization.

Rates and Bracket Freedom Under the Shared Personal Income Tax

As part of the 1991 federal budget, Ottawa appears willing to entertain the notion that the provinces that are signatories to the tax collection agreements for the personal income tax (i.e. all provinces except Quebec, which has its own PIT) be given rate and bracket structure freedom in terms of the operations of the provincial component of the shared PIT. This is in part a defensive move because even before the 1991 budget some provinces were seriously contemplating following Quebec's lead and establishing their own separate personal income tax systems. However, it can also be viewed as an accommodating move on Ottawa's part because of the fiscal bind it has placed on provincial budgeting. Regardless of Ottawa's motives, the result is again decentralizing in that it will not only allow greater fiscal flexibility to the provinces but will also give them a greater say in the distribution of income via the tax system. I have long been in favour of replacing the current "tax on base" with a "tax on tax."[3] With some provinces currently mounting up to eight tax credits, surcharges or flat taxes within the existing shared PIT system,[4] why not give the provinces the flexibility of their own rate and bracket structures since they are approaching this in any event? Note that under such a system, Ottawa would still define what constitutes income for tax purposes.

Regional Rationalization

The federal cuts and freezes in intergovernmental transfers are also having an impact in other areas. For example, the Maritime provinces are finally thinking of rationalization across their three provinces. The only notable initiative in this area thus far has been the decision by New Brunswick to hire a Nova Scotia company to produce New Brunswick licence plates. But this is at least a beginning. The potential for reaping economies of scale is surely very significant in areas such as rationalizing the university sector, medicare, the hydro grid, government purchasing, tax harmonization, and greater control of UI (including some temporary continuing interregional subsidies). Interprovincial cooperation and integration will also begin to characterize the West. These directions are essential and, assuming we back away from the existing distortions in the transfer system, rather inevitable.

Ontario and the Federation

To underscore this point about inevitability it is important to recognize the dramatically altered role of Ontario in the federation. Some aggregate numbers are instructive here. In terms of net federal spending benefits (inflows minus outflows) for 1988, the Atlantic provinces "gain" to the tune of roughly $3,000 per capita for New Brunswick and over $5,000 per capita in P.E.I. Manitoba and Saskatchewan are not that far behind either. Alberta leads the way in terms of per capita contributions on the part of the three have or "contributing" provinces. However, in terms of overall dollar flows the roughly $1,000 per capita for Ontario translates into an outflow not far off the $9.7 billion mark (i.e. the value of the forecast Ontario deficit). I am not suggesting that such calculations have much to commend them in terms of assessing who benefits from the Canadian federation. However, they do provide a convenient backdrop for focusing on the implications of the Ontario budget for the Canadian economy.[5]

Is Ontario's Tax Base Migrating South?

Ontario is in rough economic shape. High interest rates and an overvalued dollar have taken (and are still taking) their toll in terms of manufacturing plants, let alone jobs. Cross-border shopping is becoming endemic. Ontario's welfare rolls are mushrooming. Overlaying all of this is a forecast doubling of Ontario's debt—essentially from $40 billion to $80 billion over the next four years. Even after four years, the projected Ontario deficit will be roughly $7 billion. Thus, some further tax hikes are probably waiting in the wings. However, by some measures Ontario is already the most taxed jurisdiction in the country.

Is Ontario putting its tax base at risk? At what point will the ongoing southward shift in economic activity become a wholesale migration? One need not provide full answers to these questions in order to derive the following implication: if the industrial heartland begins to falter, the inter-regional distributional tap will of necessity be tightened. This is a further reason for Canada East and Canada West to pursue in earnest a needed rationalization of the design and delivery of the social envelope across their respective economic spaces.

Canada Without Quebec

The "bon voyage" movement in the Rest of Canada is predicated in part on the fact that, with Quebec out of the way, ROC can then redesign itself in its own likeness and image. However, as I have elaborated elsewhere, a rending of the nation will almost surely have a further substantial negative impact on Ontario.[6] The conception that Ontario will, in an independent ROC, continue to fund regional transfers at the former level on the one hand and bow to Western desires on the other for a Triple-E Senate (or a breakup of Ontario into two or more provinces) is surely questionable and perhaps far-fetched. At some point Ontario will be forced to act in its own self-interest. Thus, while a Canada without Quebec may be viable, it will *not* be the sort of country that many Canadians are now describing.

Ontario as Social Policy Leader

At least two other implications with respect to Ontario merit discussion. The first is that Ontario appears determined to use its tax base to become Canada's social policy leader. As long as Quebec was the leader (or before this, Saskatchewan), New Brunswick might contemplate similar initiatives, although if the tax price were too high that would be the end of the story. Not so with Ontario as the social policy leader. Here, Section 36 of the constitution (equalization, correcting regional disparities, equality of opportunity) will begin to enter the game and Ottawa will soon find itself pressured to ensure that all Canadians have access to the same level of public goods and services as Ontarians. Either the federal government will be forced to abandon its deficit reduction strategy or Canada will begin to see a divergence in the social policy envelope on a regional basis (which in turn might trigger its own set of adjustments such as in-migration to Ontario).

What Does Ontario Want?

Ontario has not bought into Ottawa's view of appropriate macro policy (nor, for that matter, have I).[7] Nor has it accepted Ottawa's interpretation of competitiveness, which Ontario interprets as little more than buying into the American creed! Phrased somewhat differently, Ontario refuses to go the "low wage, low tax, low transfer" route. Presumably its sights are set on replicating the policies of the social democracies of Europe which are "high wage, high tax, high transfer" states and tend to embody a close working relationship among business, labour and government. This is a very tall order, particularly with regard to getting business on side, in light of Ontario's recent budget.

Again, I do not want to predict whether Ontario will succeed in this endeavour, only that it will give it a try. What this will imply, however, is that Ontario will want control over a lot of new levers in order to frame a comprehensive industrial strategy. For example, it will have to integrate fully its social and economic policy, and for this it will need influence in terms of retraining, unemployment insurance, and research and development, along with greater flexibility on the tax side. Thus, strange as it might at first appear, my prediction is that Ontario will find itself in the forefront of the decentralist movement in the country.

Conclusion

What Does Ottawa Want?

Is there more to Ottawa's agenda on the interprovincial front than deficit reduction? I do not know the answer to that but let me propose the following scenario. Ottawa is fed up with lack of visibility and lack of accountability with regard to the federal-provincial transfer system. This is becoming particularly evident in the ongoing constitutional crisis where the federal view is that individual Canadians do not attach sufficient importance to the social policy role of Ottawa in their lives. One solution, therefore, is to convert aspects of the federal transfer system into the social policy equivalent of the Canadian Charter of Rights and Freedoms, i.e. to begin to *bypass* the provinces and make direct payments to citizens.

The social programme where this will become most evident is the Canada Assistance Plan. The old regime cannot be resurrected without dramatically increasing the flow of funds to the three have provinces. I do not think that this is in store, and therefore I attach some credence to the rumour that Ottawa will replace CAP with a dramatically enhanced child tax credit, leaving the provinces to top this up with provisions for adults. The obvious counterpart to this is the establishment of student education vouchers for post-secondary education that are usable anywhere in Canada (and perhaps day care vouchers as well, once Ottawa's fiscal position strengthens). The provinces have never been enthusiastic about vouchers, but vouchers will probably be viewed quite favourably if the alternative is the cash component of EPF falling toward zero. I do not think that Ottawa has much interest in becoming involved in the management of medicare, although it will insist on principles relating to portability, accessibility, and so on. My prediction here is that Ottawa will transfer a few equalized tax points to the provinces, thereby effectively scuttling EPF.

In sum then, I can visualize a process whereby Ottawa restructures the federal-provincial transfer system away from the provinces and toward direct transfers to citizens. The *quid pro quo* for the have-not provinces will be an enhanced equalization system (which would become the only federal-provincial transfer) and, for the have provinces, an enhanced tax point transfer. Presumably, however, the overall package will still place fiscal pressure on the provinces. And if Ottawa is as attached to freeing up the Canadian economic union as it suggests, then the natural corollary will be to adopt the Macdonald Commission recommendation and leave *all* place prosperity activities, apart from equalization, to the provinces.

The "Let's Equalize Everything" Alternative

At the opposite end of the spectrum is the possibility that Ottawa could follow a strategy more in keeping with the typical Canadian approach to the social envelope—to introduce an equalization component not only into all social programs but into line departments as well (as noted earlier, this is what Ottawa has done with the Canada Assistance Plan). But this could be taken further, for example by introducing a "fiscal needs" component into CAP whereby the federal share of CAP funding would depend on, say, the rate of unemployment in the provinces.

There are two problems with this approach. First, it runs counter to the notion that this time around attention has to be paid to the economic viability of any reconstituted Canada. Second, this approach has failed miserably in terms of producing tangible benefits. It is place prosperity writ large, allowing virtually every federal program or department to become involved in the redistributive game. One cannot follow this pattern and also recommend enhancing the internal economic union because these policies run counter to an economic union. I hope that past experience and global imperatives have put an end to this approach to policy making, but one never can be sure.

A Social Charter?

All of this leads in the direction of considering whether Canada ought to introduce a social charter as an integral part of its new constitutional proposals. It is true that the existing federal-provincial transfer system is in a shambles and one can reasonably expect the poorer provinces to insist on some renewed commitment on this front before accepting any reconstituted federation. A social charter offers one way to approach all of this.

I do not think, however, that there is a genuine desire on the part of Canadians to entrust social policy to the courts via some version of a justiciable social charter. More likely, the solution will be an expanded version of Section 36 (which deals with equalization payments and equality of opportunity across regions). Nonetheless, this area has very powerful symbolic dimensions because, as noted earlier, much of the glue that binds Canada together is social policy glue. At the very least, given the disintegration of the existing framework, if Ottawa wants to avoid pressures for a social charter it is going to have to propose a stable framework for federal-provincial transfers leading to the spring 1992 renegotiation of the quinquennial fiscal arrangements.

Notes

[1] Courchene, Thomas J., *In Praise of Renewed Federalism* (Toronto: C.D. Howe Research Institute, 1991).

[2] Newfoundland Royal Commission on Employment and Unemployment, *Building On Our Strengths* (St. John's: Queen's Printer, 1982). This is generally referred to as the House Report, after its Chairperson, Douglas House.

[3] Ontario Economic Council, *A Separate Personal Income Tax For Ontario: An Ontario Economic Council Position Paper* (Toronto: Ontario Economic Council, 1981).

[4] Courchene, Thomas J. and Arthur E. Stewart, "Provincial Personal Income Taxation and the Future of the Tax Collection Agreements," in Mel McMillan (ed.), *Provincial Finances: Plaudits, Problems and Prospects* (Toronto: Canadian Tax Foundation, 1991), pp. 266-300.

[5] Horry, Isabel, and Michael A. Walker, *Government Spending Facts* (Vancouver: The Fraser Institute, 1991), table 3.7.

[6] Courchene, *In Praise of Renewed Federalism*.

[7] Courchene, Thomas J., "Zero Means Almost Nothing: Towards a Preferable Inflation and Macroeconomic Policy," *Queen's Quarterly*, vol. 97, No. 4 (Winter, 1990), pp. 543-561.

Decentralization:
The External Dimension

Charles F. Doran

TO MOST AMERICANS, ENGLISH CANADA and Quebec seem like an affluent, extremely well-educated couple locked in a marriage dispute. After many years of marriage they contemplate divorce. The American impulse is to say, "But why? You already have everything."

To Quebec the Americans say, "You already are a *société distincte*. You already have won the revolution. Why risk its benefits?"

To English Canada the comment is, "Value your companion, for the union is worth the sacrifice."

Americans want Canadians, whatever their language or ethnic background, to consider what economists call opportunity costs—namely, what life will be like for each polity after the divorce. What Americans would like to recommend to Canada is a good family counsellor. Most Americans, wiser than I, know better than to allow themselves to be enticed into such a perilous role. This seems all the more appropriate since the *fédéralistes* in Quebec want to give *une dernière chance au reste du Canada* [a last chance to the rest of Canada].

Let me set out the ground rules of this discussion. First, process has already prejudged outcome. Quebec already knows that insofar as it wishes and as it proceeds by democratic vote, it can declare autonomy immediately. In a sense, that takes all the fun out of the struggle. I now see that there are diverse views at this symposium regarding the issue of democratic procedure, some of which I'm sure are tactical, but some of which may be deeper and thus cast a long shadow in the sense of the significance of the outcome.

Second, the struggle is really internal to Quebec. I would say that the struggle is really internal to francophone Canada if I were not aware that 20 per cent of the francophone population in Canada lies outside Quebec's borders in places like New Brunswick, Manitoba, and southern Ontario. But in my view, Canada's future will largely be determined in Quebec during the next two years. English Canada is neither united enough nor administratively and politically capable of mounting a full-scale response to the Allaire report, which is the most important document in Canada since patriation of the Constitution.

Third, the United States would prefer to see a strong and united Canada. There is no doubt about that. But the United States can live with virtually any outcome that Quebec and Ottawa can devise. What the United States wants is for Quebeckers and for all Canadians to be reasonably happy. That will make life next door easier. Hedonism is not written into the Canadian Constitution as it is into the American Declaration of Independence. Americans worry that deep decentralization or, for that matter, a complete break, will fail to bring happiness either to Quebec or to English Canada.

Set against this background, what I propose to comment on is the following question. How will deep decentralization, or a complete break, affect the *external capacity* of Quebec and English Canada to defend and further the interests of their citizens? This may seem like a redundant question since, regardless of state size, virtually all governments have a seat in the UN General Assembly, for example, and all have a single vote. Foreign policy may look to some like a constant across all states. Sovereignty is sovereignty. Or, in the light of interdependence, the lack of sovereignty in one place is precisely the lack of sovereignty elsewhere. But let us examine this question of foreign policy capacity and citizen interests more closely.

Size and Foreign Policy Capacity

Canada is presently a country of 25 million people, ranking it among the less populated states. But its huge territory and large GNP place it among the major industrial states of the world. Suppose it were broken up. Quebec with some six million people would be smaller than the metropolitan area of Chicago. Without Quebec, English Canada would shrink to the size of some of the smaller European states.

The first casualty would be Canada's dropping out of the Club of Seven advanced industrial summit countries. Does this matter, apart from the prestige associated with "a seat at the table?" I submit that loss of membership does matter to Canadians since all issues of political and economic substance are discussed at these summits.

Not to be involved means that one is "outside the loop," that one does not get the same type of direct information. The capacity to score points on monetary policy or in the creation of defensive coalitions is a function of being directly involved when policies are discussed and decisions are made. The average citizen may not think that membership in the Club of Seven matters, since one cannot eat prestige. But when it comes to whether interest rates affecting the purchase of a house or car are a percent or two lower or higher, the capacity to influence decisions that ultimately affect those interest rate policies becomes a matter of obvious significance.

Part of the reason that Quebec nationalists seek independence is that they want Quebec to be less dependent upon its external political environment including Ottawa, other Canadian provinces, the United States, and the rest of the international system. But would Quebec be less dependent or more dependent after a declaration of sovereignty? I believe that Quebec will be more subject to political manipulation and to actual economic dependence following autonomy. The same of course would be true for English Canada on a proportionate basis.

At present Ottawa can mediate between external rivals and competitors on the one hand, and the provinces, including Quebec, on the other. This mediation takes a number of paths. Canada as a single unit has enough clout to protect its interests and to demand visibility on the global stage. It cannot be ignored on most issues that will affect the individual provinces. It combines economic weight with a defence capability that gains it entrance to most international circles. Because of its size it can afford to devote substantial resources to its diplomatic efforts.

Mediation also occurs through a screening effect. The activities of the provinces, including their industrial policies, are not looked at with quite the same intensity by the international community when they are part of the larger Canadian polity, where their effects tend to get averaged into the overall Canadian way of doing things. But in isolation, both English Canada and Quebec will be exposed to a much finer scrutiny before the GATT and with respect to all individual treaty obligations. The smaller units will be expected to comply more punctiliously than at present, with terms that may be more onerous because less coordinated Canadian capability has underwritten their negotiation.

Small is not beautiful in world politics. There is no reason to believe that relations *per se* between Washington and English Canada, and Washington and Quebec, would be of lesser quality than at present. But if Canadians believe they are ignored now, with a population of 25 million and an economic product of corresponding size, what will the situation be with a population of under 20 million and under 7 million, respectively?

Other governments unwilling to take the long view may not be prepared to treat the smaller Canadian and Quebec entities so lightly. Mr. Trudeau and his cabinet colleagues attempted valiantly to make the notion of the Third Option work, i.e. to broaden ties with Europe through the so-called contractual link, and to use Europe and Japan as counterweights to the United States. The Third Option failed not because it was badly conceived or even badly implemented; it failed because Canada did not have enough overall weight either economically or politically to cause Europe and Japan to alter their own interests and foreign policy paths. They saw no advantages to themselves in the arrangement that they could not already obtain from Canada on less costly terms.

Some discussion now occurs in Quebec circles about using France as a counterweight to both English Canada and the United States. In concept, once again, the notion is attractive from the Quebec nationalist point of view. Relations between Quebec government officials and France are certainly cordial. In a recent article in *Le Figaro* entitled (what else?) "Vive le Québec libre!" the assertion was made that France would be the first to recognize an independent Quebec. But for France to become a more important factor in the economic and political life of Quebec, several things would have to occur.

France would need to have sufficient room for manoeuvre to pursue policies within the European Community that might conceivably differ substantially from those of, for example, Britain and Germany. Likewise, France would have to be prepared to put Quebec interests in front of its interests with the much larger English Canada and with the United States. Is there any reason to believe that the outcome would be much different than for that of the Third Option *vis-à-vis* Canada as a whole? Proponents might suggest that ties of a common language and culture ought to be worth something. In practice France, with its own view of its culture and its linguistic purity, is likely to demand much more than empathy from an autonomous Quebec if France is to be counted on in any form of high-risk coalition formation in the future.

The problem for both a separate English Canada and a separate Quebec is that, notwithstanding events in Yugoslavia and in the Soviet Union where political conditions have been very different from those in Canada, the world is moving not in the devolutionary direction but in its opposite. Witness the effort of Austria and Sweden, two smaller European countries, to become members of the European Community, an entity that has as its avowed goal the political amalgamation of all of Europe, not its segregation into national and autonomous units. Even Switzerland, with its legendary aloofness, has seen fit to move closer to the Community. Among advanced industrial market oriented countries without a communist legacy, international integration is a much stronger force than fragmentation.

Economies of scale and the commercial dangers of "border risk" are such that countries in the late twentieth century do not seem to believe that they can afford the luxury of enhanced national autonomy. This does not mean that a separate English Canada and a separate Quebec could not survive economically. Much evidence suggests the contrary. The correct question is whether there would be risks and costs attached to the prospect of smaller size. How much will smaller entities have to forgo in trade or investment terms, and how much of a loss can be expected in terms of forgone wealth and economic growth? Highly successful small states like Taiwan and Hong Kong appear to thrive despite their small size. International trade theory suggests that small states are more dependent on the international trading system than large states. But that theory does not assert that small states will necessarily prosper more than bigger states. Indeed, the movement towards international integration suggests just the opposite assumption and tendency.

This brings the discussion directly into the framework of North American free trade. To my knowledge, the United States government has not made up its bureaucratic and collective political mind about what to do regarding the Canada-U.S. Free Trade Agreement (FTA) if English Canada and Quebec apply as separate members. The negotiations with Mexico currently assume that Canada will remain a single negotiating unit. If any one of the three parties is unable to proceed with the negotiations for any reason, the other two parties are permitted to proceed *by themselves*. But for the purposes of the argument here, let us assume the ideal case; namely, that should separation occur, treaties will hold firm for both Quebec and English Canada. Other possibilities less kind to Canada exist, but let's assume the most favourable case. Does extension of the FTA mean that there are no risks or costs for the smaller resulting polities? Unfortunately, this oft-made judgment is in all likelihood quite wide of the mark.

First, the FTA does not so much guarantee access to the U.S. market as guarantee a form of due process in situations where that access is denied. It guarantees that a national of the afflicted party can sit on the panel deciding whether (1) all data have been correctly presented, and (2) the trade law of the challenged state (not that of the challenger) has been properly interpreted. Depending upon one's view of these procedures, dispute resolution panels may or may not provide much confidence regarding the stability of the trading relationship.

Second, the FTA and its successor, the North American Free Trade Agreement (NAFTA), leave unsettled much that is important to trade and commerce. Large areas such as services are virtually not covered. National treatment in many areas such as defence industries, maritime trade, cultural industries (in the case of Canada), and energy is not guaranteed. Although there is provision for a more precise negotiation of subsidies (and therefore of the constraints on countervailing duties) I doubt the technical expertise and political will exist to complete these discussions. Thus large areas of trade and commerce are without coverage under the free trade agreements.

Third, suppose that a company in Ontario or Quebec decides it needs government support to survive or expand, and that most of its output goes to the United States. Such a situation could induce a challenge from the U.S. Trade Office that would severely limit entry of Canadian goods. Or suppose that New York State decided it could not count on electricity from Hydro-Québec or faced too many environmental criticisms politically from New York constituents. Investment in nuclear power plants, costly though they might be, could sharply curtail markets for Quebec hydroelectric power in the United States. A population of six million people is likely to be much more affected by such a loss of market than is New York State, which would have only to face the prospect of building a few more nuclear power plants based on newly available safety and transmission technology.

In short, small states are subject to the whims of larger markets with or without free trade agreements that attempt to remove some of the border risk. The real leverage comes from adequate political and economic size to make a difference in the decision making of the larger entity. Reductions in size carry with them the prospect of greater dependency and greater chance for manipulation.

Decentralization and External Relations

So far we have not said or implied much regarding the impact of deep decentralization on the capacity to carry out external relations and to defend the interests of constituents *vis-à-vis* other governments. Some proposals envision a common foreign policy untouched by decentralization elsewhere in government. Other proposals imply a "slippery slope" in which decentralization in the domestic economy and administration must eventually shift to decentralization in the functions of foreign policy as well. Whatever the outcome here, several observations about impacts may be of some help as these changes are contemplated.

First, for efficiency of government to be preserved, Canada must somehow retain a single voice in its expression of policy in Washington. If decentralization were to involve representation by the major provinces in Washington along with that of Ottawa, Washington would quickly suffer from information overload. In the end the various interests would be separated and played off against each other. Canadian citizens would end up the losers.

Second, the problem with decentralization seen from outside is the question of whether international agreements would be faithfully and completely honoured by all regional or provincial groupings. That such doubts could even be raised suggests that divided internal sovereignty has external implications not just for the United States but for every foreign government dealing with Canada. If anything, a Japan or a Germany is likely to be more concerned with questions of reliability than the United States. Given the desire to diversify trade and commercial links, the states most necessary to the process may be the ones most put off by the uncertainties inherent in deep decentralization.

Third, there is some anxiety externally that deep decentralization really means tying the hands of Ottawa in terms of spending and the raising of taxes. Insofar as this is true, Canadian foreign policy could not but be affected by a more circumscribed Ottawa. Canada will be less able to undertake large external projects. It will not be able to obligate its constituents in the same way as in the past. What all of this could lead to is a "hollowing out" of Canadian foreign policy.

Notwithstanding each of these concerns, the effects of decentralization on Canadian foreign policy conduct are likely to be less far-reaching than the effects of a breakup of the country. In each case the measure is the effect on the capacity to defend or further the interests of individual constituents. Foreign policy conduct is not just some type of add-on not very relevant to the larger interests of a constituency. Especially for a country as heavily involved in trade and commerce as Canada, the external dimension requires consideration not unlike the consideration given to internal administration and decision making.

Democracy and Secession

For outsiders, one of the traits that makes all of Canadian society, both anglophone and francophone, distinctive as opposed to distinct is that it has accepted civilized rules of dialogue. More particularly, it has insisted scrupulously on democratic procedure. A reason why Americans have looked upon the debate over the Quebec role with an appropriate aloofness is that these rules of democratic procedure seemed entrenched. The statements by René Lésvesque regarding a commitment to the democratic process encouraged Americans to dissociate themselves from the Canadian debate, even though most of them disagreed with the nationalist platform of the Parti Québécois. Since nobody can predict what a more active American role might entail, this dissociation is in the interest of all the parties to the debate.

Two ground rules for the dialogue continue to be essential. First, all the actors ought to reaffirm their commitment to the democratic process in all decision making. This does not mean they have determined what kind of majority is acceptable for asserting secession. Each participant in the debate may find postponement of this issue tactically advantageous. But once the appropriate type of majority is determined, both Ottawa and Quebec City ought to reaffirm the commitment to abide by majority rule. In 1991, not to accept that Quebec has a democratic right of secession means that the referendum in 1980 was an exercise in absurdity, since in this view (i.e. that no right of secession existed), a "yes" vote would not have been acknowledged as valid.

To attempt to deny a democratically-chosen decision to secede is to assert that Quebec nationalists have misled themselves and their constituents for at least two decades. It also means that those who trusted in democratic procedure in Quebec will now be encouraged to reject it and possibly to consider non-democratic alternatives, some of which may be illegal. This will set back the cause of democracy in North America and world-wide, especially since democratic procedure is currently being appealed to in other world contexts of secession, even where there is no tradition of democratic rule. Instability and violence have been avoided throughout most of the history of the Quebec nationalist experience. Adherence to democratic principle is the best guarantee that participants in this dialogue will continue to rely on civilized means to determine whether Quebec remains in Confederation.

Second, the matter of boundaries is hotly controversial. Most Quebeckers have long assumed that the boundaries of the province are formally delineated. But since some of these boundaries were determined by the Crown as late as the latter nineteenth century and were not always a part of Lower Canada, and since some of the areas in question are claimed by native peoples, a court might decide that an independent Quebec would encompass a smaller area than at present. Such a strategy of raising disputed boundaries might also be regarded as a way of swaying opinion in Quebec against the independence option. But the strategy could back-fire. It could inflame opinion, especially among the extreme nationalists. If the appropriate court to decide these matters were the Canadian Supreme Court rather than an international court, again Quebec nationalists might noisily object. Because of the emotional content of these border matters, all participants ought to proceed with great political caution and legal care. Ottawa can best serve the cause of "peace, order, and good government" when all the actors believe that the government has treated them and their interests fairly.

Conclusions

This short paper does not pretend to present a complete picture of all aspects of structural change in Canada. English Canada and Quebec may well find some goals so compelling that all else is to be ignored in the final judgment. On the other hand, to treat the external dimension as a constant, as though structural change will have no effect on foreign policy conduct, is a large error.

Mackenzie King allegedly told the young Lester Pearson, "In the course of human history far more has been accomplished for the welfare and the progress of mankind in preventing bad actions than in doing good ones."[1] That is something of the spirit in which these modest comments on the truly monumental changes now contemplated in Canada have been offered by a sympathetic and interested friend.

Notes

[1] Peter C. Newman, *The Distemper of our Times* (Toronto: McClelland & Stewart, 1968), p. 52.

The International Relations of Provinces and States: Federalism in an Age of Economic Interdependence

Earl H. Fry

Canada's Unity Crisis: A U.S. Perspective

BILL 150 HAS BEEN INTRODUCED in Quebec's National Assembly, stating that Quebec has two political options: renewed federalism or sovereignty. Premier Robert Bourassa has visited Washington to emphasize his support for the renewed federalism option. Earlier, Jacques Parizeau made his trek to Washington to explain why sovereignty was the best option, and why this course of action would harm neither the strategic nor the business interests of the United States.

How is Canada's current crisis in constitutionalism, unity, and federalism perceived in the United States? As is common, few Americans are even aware of what is occurring in Canada. Far more Americans have heard of Lake Louise than Lake Meech. Not one in 10,000 would have any idea of what type of animal is the Reform Party or the Bloc Québécois. Even our surveys of American college students still indicate that they are very ignorant of things Canadian.

Among the so-called attentive public in the United States, the Atlantic Council of the United States is holding a series of meetings on the challenges facing Canada. The Council on Foreign Relations may also put together a study group, and the New York-based Americas Society is also interested, but much of its attention has recently been focused on the proposed North American Free Trade Agreement (NAFTA). The Association for Canadian Studies in the United States (ACSUS) will be the one place south of the 49th parallel where there will be an orgy of presentations on Canadian topics; over 300 papers will be presented at its biennial conference in Boston, several dealing with the current constitutional crisis. As for the U.S. State Department, it is quite aware of what is transpiring and has devoted significant resources to studying the current Canadian situation. Moreover, the *New York Times*, the *Washington Post*, and the *Wall Street Journal* occasionally carry an article devoted to Canada. In overall perspective, however, there is not a great deal of interest among the rank-and-file population in what is transpiring in Canada—which, unfortunately, is the normal state of affairs in the bilateral relationship.

On the other hand, one should not construe from this that the U.S. business community, with significant investments in Canada, is not concerned about Canada's predicament. Corporate boardrooms do not like uncertainty, and there is considerable uncertainty in Canada today; uncertainty regarding not only unity, but also fiscal policies, taxation, and management-labour relations.

Ironically, if the NAFTA is implemented, and I hope it will be, we will unite economically not only 360 million people with a combined gross national product of US$6 trillion, but also the world's first, second and fourth-ranked debtor countries. Moreover, we will bring together three nations burdened with among the largest current account deficits anywhere around the globe. And even though the United States faces enormous economic challenges in terms of government and trade deficits and huge external debts, I believe that the situation is much more severe in Canada, especially in terms of federal and provincial government indebtedness, the heavy burden of interest payments linked to these deficits, and Canada's onerous external debt obligations. These economic and fiscal problems may well exacerbate efforts to forge a renewed system of federalism in Canada over the next year and a half.

Federalism's Prominent Role in the 1990s

Federalism is a controversial concept in the somewhat chaotic global landscape of the 1990s. In an era when the nations of the European Community are harmonizing policies in order to take advantage of growing regional and international economic interdependence, several federal systems are moving in the opposite direction and are in danger of breaking apart. In Yugoslavia, the federal system composed of six republics may be on the verge of disintegration. In the Soviet Union, Mikhail Gorbachev was temporarily deposed on the eve of enacting a national treaty which would have established a new federation of sovereign states and put in place a modified system of sovereignty-association. Yet even before the failed coup, six of the Soviet Union's 15 republics—the three Baltic states plus Georgia, Armenia, and Moldavia—had refused to acquiesce in this new arrangement. Gorbachev insisted that if these recalcitrant republics did not join the revised union, they would be deprived of the most favoured nation (MFN) treatment which would have been a hallmark of the new sovereignty-association system. Deprived of MFN status, these six republics would have been forced to pay hard currency for energy and other supplies at world prices, making it much more difficult for them to survive outside the Soviet economic system.[1]

Those who criticize federalism maintain that the constitutional division of authority between central and regional governments provides sustenance for discontent in areas where ethnic and religious tensions are high. They add that in a global system which is increasingly interdependent in the economic, resource, energy, and environmental spheres, federalism has become a breeding ground for tribalistic impulses which are anathema to growing cooperative ties that transcend national borders.

In the case of the Soviet Union and Yugoslavia, I reject the notion that federalism is directly at fault. For much of the post-World War II period, these two nations had federal systems in name only. Particularly in the case of the Soviet Union, a sprawling empire which encompassed 11 time zones and which was only 50 per cent Russian, its 100 or so major ethnic groups were held together through coercion and ideology.

On the other hand, the most active non-central governmental actors in an increasingly interdependent world happen to be those found in federal systems. Moreover, among the federal systems scattered around the globe, Canadian provincial and U.S. state governments are the leaders in forging new economic links which transcend national borders. These two North American nations have also forged the largest and most intricate bilateral trading and investment relationship in the world. If the more than $200 billion in annual transborder trade in goods and services is to continue to grow, the Canada-U.S. Free Trade Agreement (FTA) must be faithfully implemented by the end of the 1990s and workable solutions found to such nagging problems as trade-distorting subsidies and dispute settlement procedures and mechanisms. Such solutions will depend not only on the good will of leaders in Ottawa and Washington, D.C., but also in the capitals of the 50 American states and the ten Canadian provinces.[2] Moreover, if a tripartite North American Free Trade Area (NAFTA) is created over the next few years, the 31 Mexican states (particularly the six states which border on the United States and which are home to most of the *maquiladora* facilities) may become significant actors in facilitating or hampering continental economic links.

States and Provinces as International Economic Actors

The FTA binds Canada into an economic relationship with a nation whose population and economy are approximately ten times larger. Indeed, the United States has one state, California, that surpasses Canada both in population and in economic production. By the same token, Canada has one province, Ontario, which during the 1980s was a larger recipient of U.S. exports than Japan.

To illustrate the economic prowess of these non-central government actors, consider the following. If one were to rank the 25 leading nations in the world by GNP, one could insert ten states and two provinces; among the top 50 nations, 33 states and four provinces; and among the top 75 nations, all 50 states and nine of the 10 provinces. California, with its 30 million people, produces more agricultural goods than over 90 per cent of the world's nation-states. It also enters the 1990s with a $700 billion annual gross state product and would rank as the eighth largest country globally. New York is not far behind with its top ten ranking, and Texas alone has twice the production base of neighbouring Mexico.

The immense size of some of the state and provincial governments also impacts dramatically on both national and international economic policies. For example, California faces in the 1991-92 fiscal year a government deficit of US$14 billion, a sum larger than the general fund budgets of 47 of the 50 states. Ontario will face a deficit of CAN$9.7 billion. Both governments will enact new taxes which will increase the cost of doing business and will affect corporate competitiveness both at home and abroad. Ironically, before the recent economic downturn along the two U.S. coasts and in central Canada, the rapid economic growth of California and Ontario made it difficult for the national central banks to lower interest rates, even though other parts of the United States and Canada were suffering from economic downturns.

Furthermore, the annual budgets of entities such as California and Ontario are surpassed by only a handful of national governments around the world. To put this purchasing power in perspective, California's budget is four times greater than that of the Philippines, a nation with 56 million people. At the municipal level, New York City's annual budget is also twice as large as that of the Philippines, and the four-county Greater Los Angeles metropolitan area, with an annual production of goods and services approaching $300 billion, ranks as the twelfth largest economic power in the world ahead of India, Australia, and Switzerland.

In addition, the political influence of individual non-central governments and their federal representatives should not be underestimated. In the 1992 congressional elections, California will elect nearly one of every eight members of the U.S. House of Representatives, more than the combined representation of 21 other states. California will also control 54 of the 270 electoral college votes needed to elect the President of the United States (20 per cent). Ontario's influence on the Canadian political system is even more dominant, for it elects one-third of the seats in the House of Commons. Because of the need to cater to local constituencies, and in view of the diversity among non-central units in such nations as Canada and the United States (which rank globally as the second and fourth largest in land mass), pressure intensifies for the development of subnational industrial policies which protect and enhance the economic interests of local constituencies. At times, these policies may even differ from those of national capitals.[3]

To illustrate this point, one should keep in mind that economic development prospects differ dramatically from one non-central government to the next. In Canada, Ontario alone is responsible for 40 per cent of Canada's gross national product and manufacturing exports. Ontario and its eastern neighbour Quebec jointly account for over 60 per cent of the nation's population and productivity, and more than 55 per cent of all exports. Moreover, Ontario consistently maintains an unemployment rate far below the national average, whereas the four Atlantic provinces of New Brunswick, Nova Scotia, Prince Edward Island, and Newfoundland suffer from chronically high unemployment rates. The western provinces of British Columbia, Alberta, Saskatchewan, and Manitoba have traditionally endured the boom-and-bust cycles associated with resource-dependent economies.

In the United States, the per capita income in Connecticut is more than twice as great as that in Mississippi.[4] Land in several of the Western states is also predominantly owned by the federal government, with federal ownership ranging from 30 per cent in Montana to 79 per cent in Nevada.

During a substantial portion of the 1980s, the economic development rate of the Atlantic and Pacific coast states was triple that of the interior states, prompting one U.S. senator to warn that the nation was sliding toward "two Americas: flourishing, urban coastlines and a declining rural heartland."[5] In particular, those states that are heavily dependent on agriculture, resource extraction, and traditional industries suffered significant economic upheavals during the past decade. In 1987, for example, the United States created almost three million (net) new jobs, most of which were "bicoastal" employment opportunities, while Dallas, Texas, lost 39,000 jobs and several Mountain and Plains states experienced a net outflow of workers.[6] During all or part of the 1980s, eleven states, mostly from the interior, actually lost population.

Thus, in view of the wide variety of economic profiles present at the subnational level, it should not be surprising that decisions rendered in the foreign economic policy realm may be viewed differently by non-central governments within the same nation. In the case of the FTA, members of the U.S. Congress voted overwhelmingly in favour of the pact. Near the end of the negotiating process, however, a group of 21 senators mostly from the Western states signed a petition asking for major changes in the accord because they perceived that Canada would have a noticeable advantage in transborder trade in natural resources. In Canada, provincial representatives were consulted on a monthly basis during the negotiating process, and their influence on Ottawa's final proposals regarding such issues as subsidies, government procurement, and investment restrictions was far greater than the influence wielded by their state counterparts over Washington's final set of proposals.[7] Without any doubt, the capacity of U.S. and Canadian non-central governments to influence future international commerce across the 49th parallel, whether positively or negatively, should not be underestimated.

The Economic Policies of the States and Provinces

Reverse Investment Programs

In 1970, four American states had opened offices overseas for the purpose of attracting foreign investment and enhancing trade and tourism opportunities. In 1991, 43 states were operating more than 160 offices abroad. During the same period, the number of states having international trade and development programs increased from 15 to 49.

In Canada, seven of the ten provinces have opened more than 50 offices abroad, with Quebec alone maintaining 26 international bureaus. Proportionally, the number of provincial overseas offices is far higher than those maintained by the U.S. states. Many of the provinces' expenditures on overseas activities are not in the public domain, but it is generally accepted that they are more actively involved than most of the American states. Indeed, in the mid-1980s, the province of Alberta sponsored more international trade missions annually than the 13 U.S. Western states combined.[8] Alberta and Quebec have also created separate Departments of International Trade.[9]

Foreign direct investment is responsible for more than six million jobs in North America, and the states and provinces have been willing to spend hundreds of millions of dollars annually in incentive packages to attract this investment. When Volkswagen announced in the mid-1970s that it was searching for a plant location in the United States, 35 states expressed a strong interest. Pennsylvania finally landed the VW facility, but because of the intense bidding war among the states, officials in Harrisburg had to offer an incentive package worth more than $70 million to the German-based transnational corporation. Ironically, only a decade later VW closed this assembly plant in Pennsylvania, although the company will continue to collect benefits from the state's incentive package into the 21st century.

Thirty-nine states also entered the bidding war for the Nissan Motor Company's proposed truck assembly plant. Tennessee won the contest with an incentive package valued at US$66 million. The taxpayers of Kentucky will provide US$325 million in incentives to Toyota over a

20-year period in order to entice that Japanese firm to construct its new automobile assembly plant in Georgetown.[10]

Often in concert with Ottawa, Canadian provincial governments have also provided hundreds of millions of dollars in incentives to U.S. and Asian auto makers for the establishment of assembly plants. Subsidies abound. The Alberta government, for example, provided a CAN$103 million loan guarantee to Magnesium Company of Canada Ltd. to help develop new technology for magnesium processing. Unfortunately, the company's Alberta plant has now been closed.[11]

Export Promotion

Almost all states and provinces now provide significant export assistance to small and medium-sized firms. For example, the American states spent US$62 million staffing and maintaining their trade departments in 1988, almost double the 1984 expenditures. This figure, however, may be less than the combined spending of just four Canadian provinces: Ontario, Quebec, Alberta, and British Columbia.[12] Twenty-seven states have also passed legislation to implement some form of export financing, and state and local governments are collectively spending more money to promote export activity than the federal government. The California Export Finance Office (CEFO) has emerged as a leader in providing loan guarantees to smaller enterprises, and from its inception in 1985 through mid-1990 CEFO guaranteed US$51 million in loans, generating US$260 million in new export sales.[13]

Cooperation and Competition

To enhance cooperative ties and facilitate economic linkages, several non-central governments have strengthened relations with their counterparts across the 49th parallel. Eleven New England governors and Eastern Canadian premiers have met annually since 1973 and have established a broad range of institutional agreements. For example, at the 1990 annual meeting of this group held in Connecticut, the leaders spent time on the regional ramifications of the Canada-U.S. Free Trade Agreement and solutions to the acid rain problem. Governors from eight states and premiers from two provinces have agreed on a charter to protect water rights in the Great Lakes.[14] Representatives of Alaska, British Columbia, and the Yukon also meet on a regular basis, as do officials of several other provinces and border states. Tourism is also an area where cooperation among non-central units is not unusual. This is a multibillion dollar industry with record numbers of foreign visitors coming to North America in 1990 and again in 1991.[15] The state of Washington and the province of British Columbia have agreed to set aside US$75,000 each for joint advertising campaigns. The New England governors and Eastern Canadian premiers also work together to entice residents from North America and abroad to visit their region. These regional contacts may also lead to special transborder economic arrangements, as illustrated by the Quebec government's agreement with New York and some of the New England states to export electricity worth more than US$30 billion over the next two decades.

On the other hand, economic competition among state and provincial governments is at times very intense, and beggar-thy-neighbour tactics are not uncommon. For example, Indiana business development officers spend time in Michigan; Missouri's governor meets with business representatives in Illinois; North Dakota officials host receptions for businesses in Manitoba; and Ottawa works with various provincial governments to entice firms to locate in Canada instead of in neighbouring U.S. border states.[16] A classic instance of cross-border competition occurred several years ago when an incentive package worth almost CAN$70 million was pieced together by Ontario and Ottawa in order to entice Ford to locate a new plant in Ontario instead of Ohio.[17] During the FTA negotiations, some of the most bitter disputes involved arguments among bordering states and provinces sharing similar natural resource bases. These included major disagreements over the treatment in the FTA of potatoes, corn, wheat, raspberries, oil, natural gas, timber, and fish.

Subnational Industrial Policies

State and provincial governments are clearly in the process of developing their own industrial policies and this will certainly have an impact on future trade and investment activity across the 49th parallel. In the United States, two dozen states are now directly involved in the venture capital game, committing in excess of US$300 million for projects over the past few years. State agencies also provide low-interest loans and technical managerial assistance, as well as help in securing private financing. As an illustration, the Connecticut Product Development Corporation has invested more than

US$12 million in approximately 60 small businesses. The state receives a five per cent royalty on products sold by the companies backed by this venture capital.[18] Recently, the Connecticut state government also entered into a controversial agreement to purchase 47 per cent of the equity in the Colt Manufacturing Company, a major supplier of automatic weapons. Pennsylvania's Ben Franklin Partnership has provided over US$80 million for state-based technology projects, and the Massachusetts Technology Development Corporation has distributed more than US$10 million in seed money.[19] In addition, several states have set up industrial parks, business incubators, and greenhouse projects (geared to the construction of special buildings to house new high-technology businesses) to spur on economic development. Thirty-eight states have also authorized the creation of enterprise zones, up from 26 in 1985. Hundreds of millions of dollars in tax breaks and other types of financial assistance are available to companies locating in these specially designated zones.[20]

In general, state governments are also much more involved than ever before in regulating businesses, whether domestic or foreign. A Conference Board study of 253 of the largest corporations in the United States reveals that 75 per cent now engage in lobbying efforts in one or more states, and nearly one-half of the companies which employ state government relations specialists have hired them since 1975. This seems to be an astute decision because at least seven times as many business-related laws are being passed by state legislatures as by the U.S. Congress.

As for Canada, most provincial governments are much more active than their state counterparts in regulating businesses. Provincial governments also own hundreds of Crown corporations and are integrally involved in most facets of the economy.[21] In addition, they provide about CAN$2 billion annually to support agricultural programs.[22] In general, provincial governments are also much more deeply in debt than their counterparts in the United States, and they view trade, reverse direct investment, and tourism as indispensable revenue sources.

Quebec, for example, is one of several provinces which sponsors an investor immigrant program. Under the provisions of this program, a prospective immigrant will be given preference if he or she is willing to bring at least CAN$700,000 in net capital and invest at least CAN$500,000 for three years or more. This investment must be made through a stockbroker and targeted at Quebec-based businesses with assets of less than

CAN$25 million. Quebec's Solidarity Fund and the Caisse de Dépot et Placement are also used to promote economic development in the province.[23] The latter organization was established in 1965 and administers the funds from 11 Quebec public pension and insurance plans. It is one of North America's largest financial institutions, with assets exceeding CAN$30 billion, and has participated in the capitalization of hundreds of Quebec companies.

Provinces such as Quebec also provide incentives to foreign investors, often in conjunction with local governments and with federal government agencies which promote regional economic development. Moreover, in an effort to maintain its francophone culture, the Quebec government provides cash bonuses, income tax cuts, interest-free loans for homes, and other inducements to families willing to have more than two children. Quebec has also entered into a special immigration agreement with Ottawa in 1991, and has its own agents who work with federal immigration officials to screen potential newcomers to the province on the basis of their knowledge of French or commitment to learn the French language.

Provinces, States, and Economic Interdependence: Concluding Observations

This paper has at times focused on some of the troubling byproducts of state and provincial activism in the domestic and international economies. At this juncture, it is important to point out that many subnational activities are positive forces for change, representing a grassroots effort to familiarize people with the challenges and opportunities in a rapidly evolving global economy. For example, the National Governors' Association is prodding its members to push for the reinstatement of foreign language proficiency as a requirement for college admission, the restoration of geography as a core subject in school curricula, the introduction of foreign language training at the elementary school level, and state-sponsored courses in international commerce for local business communities. These and other related measures should help prepare the citizenry on both sides of the 49th parallel for a truly internationalized economy.

The FTA is also a proper response to the exigencies of globalization, and trade and investment linkages continue to expand between the two North American neighbours even during the recent recession. In Canada, however, the FTA is off to a rocky start. It has been blamed for every societal ill whether real or imaginary, and a plurality of Canadians still disapprove of the accord. In the United States, most Americans have little knowledge about the FTA and or what is transpiring in U.S.-Canada economic relations, in spite of their generally friendly perception of Canada. As for the proposed NAFTA, a Gallup poll released in March 1991 indicated that 72 per cent of Americans and 66 per cent of Mexicans, but only 28 per cent of Canadians, favour a tripartite pact.

Future prospects for the FTA and NAFTA have been somewhat clouded by the failure of the Meech Lake constitutional discussions and the possibility either that Quebec will separate from the rest of Canada or that the Canadian system will become so decentralized that both North-South and East-West trade and investment linkages will be substantially weakened. Nonetheless, momentum favouring the approval of NAFTA is building in view of the extension of the fast-track authority by the U.S. Congress and the commencement of formal negotiations during the summer of 1991.

Yet in spite of the FTA, numerous trade restrictions still exist between the United States and Canada at the state and provincial levels. These include non-tariff trade barriers, trade-distorting subsidies, government procurement limitations, and investment restraints. With increased competition from across the Pacific and the Atlantic, it would seem prudent for the North American economies to rationalize and eliminate the remaining subnational-level trade constraints in their federal systems. If the barriers highlighted in this article are to be dismantled, provincial and state governments must be willing to join with Ottawa and Washington, D.C., in fine-tuning the FTA and in negotiating a comprehensive NAFTA arrangement.

Notes

This paper is an updated version of "Canada-U.S. Economic Relations: The Role of the Provinces and the States," *Business in the Contemporary World* 3 (Autumn 1990), pp. 120-126.

[1] See the *New York Times*, April 28, 1991, VI, p. 1, and the *Financial Times*, May 2, 1991, p. 2.

[2] At the 1988 annual conference of the provincial premiers, these non-central government leaders demanded "a strong provincial role" in the management of Canada-U.S. free trade, the definition of subsidies, the

development of common trade remedy laws, and the determination of dispute settlement mechanisms. The National Governors' Association has also requested that the Office of the U.S. Trade Representative consult with the states on any bilateral economic issue which impacts upon the economic well-being of the states. See the *Globe and Mail*, August 20, 1988, pp. A1 & A2.

[3] Canada has a much more decentralized system than the United States, and federalism is a far more prominent feature of Canada's political structure. As Peter Leslie observes in *Federal State, National Economy* (Toronto: University of Toronto Press, 1987), p. ix, "...the most fundamental political relationships, defining the character of Canadian society, are bound up in the structure of the federal system. It shapes them, and they shape it."

[4] The 1987 per capita income in Connecticut was US$20,980; in Mississippi US$10,204.

[5] This statement was made by Senator David Durenberger at the 1988 Minnesota Republican nominating convention. See the *St. Paul Pioneer Press Dispatch*, June 18, 1988, p. 6A.

[6] In 1987, eight of the ten most robust economies were found in coastal states, and the other two, Arizona and Nevada, depended on California for much of their growth. See *Inc.*, October 1987, pp. 76-77.

[7] This conclusion is derived from the author's interviews with representatives of the U.S. and Canadian FTA negotiating teams and with provincial and state officials who interacted with their national teams. The large provinces established special FTA task forces and produced some very sophisticated papers on the economic and social impact which dimensions of the FTA would have on their constituents. These papers were discussed with Simon Reisman and his FTA team and viewpoints were exchanged on a regular basis.

In contrast, few state representatives followed the FTA negotiations closely, and meetings between officials of the National Governors' Association and the Office of the U.S. Trade Representative were held on a very infrequent and *ad hoc* basis. On the other hand, state representatives were able to make their positions known through the U.S. Congress, whereas strict party discipline, reliance on executive federalism, and an anachronistic Senate made Canada's Parliament a poor conduit for the expression of provincial concerns. Nevertheless, the articulation of state concerns in the House of Representatives and the Senate was far less effective than the consultative mechanism worked out by the Canadian Trade Negotiator's Office and the provincial governments.

[8] This conclusion is based on a survey conducted by the author in 1986. See Earl H. Fry, "The Economic Competitiveness of the Western States and Provinces: The International Dimension," *The American Review of Canadian Studies* 16 (Autumn 1986), pp. 301-312. Since that time, however, the states have become much more active in sponsoring international missions and it is doubtful that the same results would be found in 1991.

[9] Some of the provincial export-related programs are listed in Department of External Affairs, International Trade, *Provincial Trade-Related Assistance Programs*, April 1989.

[10] *Wall Street Journal*, June 9, 1987, p. 33.

[11] *Financial Post*, April 15, 1991, p. 3.

[12] When the costs of maintaining foreign offices for trade purposes are included, it is more than likely that these four provinces spend more on trade promotion than the 50 states. See, for example, Douglas Brown's discussion of Alberta in "Canada's Provinces in the International Economy: A Survey of the Field," a paper presented at the Dartmouth Conference on Comparative Federalism, June 22-25, 1989. Also consult Ivan Bernier and André Binette, *Les provinces canadiennes et le commerce international* (Quebec City: Centre québécois des relations internationales, 1988), pp. 65-73, and *Provincial Trade-Related Assistance Programs*.

[13] *Wall Street Journal*, November 7, 1990, pp. B1 & B2.

[14] The Great Lakes Charter was signed in February 1985 by the governors of New York, Pennsylvania, Ohio, Michigan, Indiana, Illinois, Wisconsin, and Minnesota, and the premiers of Ontario and Quebec.

[15] In spite of the Gulf War and an economic downturn in several industrialized countries, the U.S. Travel and Tourism Administration expects a record 41.5 million foreign residents to visit the United States in 1991, up seven per cent from the record 38.8 million in 1990. These visitors are expected to spend US$56.9 billion in 1991, versus US$51.1 billion in 1990. See the U.S. Travel and Tourism Administration report issued on May 13, 1991.

[16] *Wall Street Journal*, February 14, 1983, pp. 1 & 11, and December 28, 1983, pp. 1 & 13.

[17] See Earl H. Fry, *Financial Invasion of the U.S.A.* (New York: McGraw-Hill, 1980), p. 146.

[18] *Christian Science Monitor*, November 20, 1984, p. 37.

[19] *Wall Street Journal*, November 9, 1987, p. 27.

[20] *Ibid.*, April 1, 1991, pp. B1 & B2.

[21] It is extremely difficult to place a dollar figure on the direct and indirect subsidies provided by the provincial governments. In 1984, Statistics Canada reported that perhaps CAN$4 billion in direct subsidies were provided by these subnational governments, a 100 per cent increase from 1980. See Bernier and Binette, p. 63. Also consult pp. 65-73 for a look at provincial programs which assist local exporters.

[22] *Globe and Mail*, May 16, 1989, p. A6.

[23] Quebec's Solidarity Fund began in 1984 with a CAN$10 million provincial government loan and CAN$6 million raised from union members. In 1990, it ranked as Quebec's single largest source of venture capital with CAN$294 million in assets and 85,000 shareholders.

Section IV

Quebec and the Independence Option

Does Globalization Make an Independent Quebec More Viable?

Robert A. Young

The Economics Of Separatism

MY TITLE POSES A QUESTION which is topical and which will be hotly debated throughout this constitutional round, both in Quebec and in the rest of Canada. Here I will outline a brief answer to it, by tackling three issues.

First, the question normally alludes to what economic consequences sovereignty might have, and highlights a new economic argument in favour of Quebec independence, which I will describe. In this context, the question may seem to contain an internal contradiction because however amorphous the concept of globalization, it commonly implies interdependence, not independence; and yet it is precisely within a more interdependent global economy that Quebec sovereigntists see fresh opportunity for autonomous manoeuvre. In contrast, I will argue that Quebec's power in negotiating the regimes within which economic forces operate would be reduced by its accession to independence.

Finally there is "viability." No one can doubt that Quebec constitutes a viable society, as it has done for decades if not centuries. On the economic front the only relevant question is the cost of sovereignty, but my concern is with the linguistic and cultural future, and with the viability of what makes the province distinctive and makes its people prepared to bear some cost in order to manage their collective affairs themselves. The justified anxiety of most Quebeckers about preserving their identity can be met, it seems to me, through constitutional reform rather than sovereignty's rupture.

There are currently two basic arguments in Quebec in support of the sovereignty option. The most familiar concerns the province's position as the homeland of the French language in North America. It holds that only an independent Quebec state armed with a full range of sovereign powers can protect and preserve the linguistic and cultural distinctiveness of francophone Quebeckers. Only through such a state can *le peuple québécois* collectively secure its common future in a turbulent world. This is an old argument and it runs deep in Québécois sentiment. Alone it has not proven powerful enough—and neither has the level of threat from Canada and elsewhere been strong enough—to generate an *indépendantiste* majority, and yet the doctrine that Quebec is distinct, that its distinction rests now on language and culture, and that Québécois are justified in using their state to defend their collective identity, commands wide support among francophone Quebeckers.

In the past, of course, economic reality has been invoked to cool off autonomist yearnings. National self-determination could be costly. In much of the debate about independence, participants on both sides have assumed an implicit trade-off between political autonomy and economic welfare. But this is changing. A new economic argument in favour of Quebec independence is being forged, and in the current national and international conjuncture it has acquired some plausibility and many adherents.

One part of the new economic argument is domestic. The Quebec economy is stronger and more dynamic than in the past. It is less dependent on Canadian markets as its foreign trade has grown fast. And the federal system, rather than supporting the province, is draining resources and inhibiting growth. Ottawa has been unable to reduce its own deficits, and the consequent burden of interest payments is huge; monetary policy, high interest rates and an overvalued dollar have inhibited growth; and Ottawa's development policies have failed, as competitive federalism has resulted in duplication, federal-provincial friction, incoherent policy, and waste.[1]

To these arguments about static losses because of the domestic political economy are added others resting on globalization. This is a vague notion, often undefined, but it generally refers to increases in international flows of capital, direct investment, trade, and labour, along with greater transnational corporate activity, often in new forms like joint ventures and strategic alliances, and a massive increase in communications and information flows worldwide. The advent of globalization means that complexes of economic activity transcend national borders. Less and less are access to markets, capital, workers, technology, and information a function of national policies. Under the GATT, for example, tariff barriers on most goods have become insignificant (in the OECD countries at least) and so Quebec manufacturers are as likely to find markets in Boston as in Toronto. Global economic activities are mediated by a range of governmental actors—cities, states, national governments, and international agencies—which have created a complex, multilevel web of treaties, agreements and norms. The power to dictate the terms under which economic agents operate has become terribly diffuse in this global economy.[2]

One implication of Canada's being enmeshed in this web of international obligations is that punitive measures against a sovereign Quebec are difficult to contemplate. As a GATT member, for instance, Quebec would enjoy guaranteed access to Canadian markets at most-favoured-nation (MFN) tariff rates. Beyond this, the ideology of global markets suggests that punitive and trade-restrictive policies hurt both countries. A Canada interfering with market forces by erecting barriers to Quebec asbestos or steel or trucking would be shooting itself in the foot by raising prices to its consumers, and rendering its own industries less competitive in the world.

In this new international environment, smaller states seem less vulnerable than they were to policy threats by larger foreign powers, and so globalization has reduced the potential losses to Quebeckers of choosing sovereignty. It has more significant implications for growth. An important aspect of globalization is freer markets and the diminished potential of old industrial policy instruments like tariffs, subsidies and protectionist regulation. The new emphasis is on innovation, adjustment, human capital formation and intrasocietal cooperation (to share information and reduce wasteful conflict). Hence—the argument runs—a small, adaptable, consensual society with a loyal business class, and with public policies tailor-made for it, is more capable of economic growth than is the same society when inserted within a larger unit where adjustment is slow, government is inefficient and conflict-ridden, and policies—because they necessarily reflect an interregional compromise—are never exactly suited to its requirements.[3] Quebeckers can sail the international waters more surely in their own snug sloop, as it were, than when stuck aboard a big top-heavy galleon whose sail can't be trimmed to the breezes of opportunity—or battened against the gales of necessity.

Returning to solid land, it is easy to find weaknesses in both of these new economic arguments. First consider transition costs. Assume Quebeckers take a majority decision in favour of sovereignty. Assume too on the part of the Rest of Canada (ROC) not only a grudging forbearance of mutually harmful measures, but also the best of goodwill. Quebec independence still will be costly to both parties. There are the initial costs of negotiating transfers of assets, debts, public employees, programs and revenue sources, and these would not be negligible, either directly or in the effects of public sector disorganization on business.

More important, though, is uncertainty. On the part of labour, this could result in a substantial exodus from the province. On the part of investors the problem is even more serious. The very internationalization of capital markets means that investors are used to considering a wide range of alternative locations, and fundamental constitutional change increases the perceived risk of placing funds in both Canada and Quebec. Public and corporate debt would be financed at a premium; more immediately, new direct investment certainly would diminish in the face of deep political uncertainty, which would exist even were aboriginal peoples and Quebec anglophones to make rapid accommodations to the new regime (and this they show little inclination to do).

Ironically, transition costs could be minimized most effectively by guaranteeing continuity in policy. Yet this would constrain the very autonomy on which the new economic arguments for sovereignty count to produce more sustained economic development. We will return to this below, but it is worth emphasizing that promises of policy continuity and mutual efforts by Quebec and ROC to manage the disengagement smoothly would not eliminate transition costs. Then again, whether these costs are supportable depends not only on their magnitude but also on the discount rate applied to the future gains arising from Quebec's superior competitiveness in the global economy.

Suppose that, within Canada, Quebec would average 2.5 per cent yearly growth in GDP over the long run, and that a sovereign Quebec would grow at 3.5 per cent each year. Suppose as well that the economy grew in a three-year transition period at rates of minus 1.5 per cent, 0 per cent and 1 per cent before getting onto the trajectory of 3.5 per cent per year growth; that is, Quebeckers gave up 8 per cent growth in the short term to get an extra 1 per cent forever. First, it is worth noting that Quebec would have recovered all lost ground by the spring of 2004. Moreover, at a discount rate of slightly under ten per cent, this would represent a perfectly rational decision. At a discount rate of five per cent, the value of the future benefits would far outweigh the short-term costs. If, however, it took six years to get onto the new 3.5 per cent trajectory, and 20 per cent of GDP growth were sacrificed in the interim, Quebec would not recover lost ground until around 2019, and its people would have to value future benefits very highly indeed to opt for sovereignty. They might do so. At issue is the future of a nation. If everyone had "normal" discount rates, very few oak trees would be planted. But this discussion shows how critical, from an economic point of view, is the assumption that a more autonomous Quebec could achieve more rapid economic growth.[4]

Confronting the Regimes

Here we return to globalization. The economic argument rests on free access to global markets by a small, consensual society able to make rapid adaptations to change in market forces. But the fundamental point to be made against this view is that the international economy is not a featureless space where free market competition reigns. World economic activity occurs within politically determined frameworks. These frameworks are called *regimes* by political scientists. The term can refer to expected patterns of interaction, norms, rules, and formal treaties supervised by transnational agencies. In any case the implication is the same: regimes established by nation-states help structure the patterns and outcomes of economic activity. They may encourage or retard trade, make certain transactions more or less profitable, and channel flows of capital, people, technology and information.

An example of a hard regime is the Coordinating Committee for Multilateral Strategic Export Controls (COCOM), which determines what products can be sold by Western firms to unfriendly countries, regardless of how much potential profit is at stake. Similarly, the GATT is a negotiated regime which conditions the flow of trade and circumscribes the actions of its signatory states. If it is understood that global economic forces operate within the framework of a complex set of negotiated agreements, Quebec's prospects as a sovereign state hinge on its position within various regimes and its capacity to protect its interests in negotiating them.

The first relevant regime is the GATT, which poses few problems. Quebec would accede to normal membership rapidly, especially were ROC supportive. As noted, Quebec would then enjoy access to Canadian markets, at a minimum, at MFN tariff rates.

But Canada and Quebec would create a bilateral regime, as discussed below, which would go far beyond the GATT and other existing multilateral agreements (such as those in civil aviation, for instance). Apart from this, Quebec's most important regime is the Canada-U.S. Free Trade Agreement, about which the Bélanger-Campeau Commission stated:

> An independent Quebec which would clearly indicate its intention to continue to participate in the movement toward freer trade on the continent should not meet with opposition from its partners; it would be incumbent upon Quebec and its partners to ensure that the mutual interests which led to the Agreement continue to prevail.

> Through its participation in GATT and the continuation of free trade with the United States, Quebec would maintain the current terms of its economic relations with the United States and the rest of the world.[5]

This, like the rest of the report, accepts as desirable the openness of Quebec to the international economy. But the sanguine assumption that Quebec could continue to be covered by the current terms of the FTA is surprising, given that the Commission's own expert consultant concluded that under any principle of succession the FTA would have to be renegotiated and also resubmitted to the GATT for approval under Article XXIV.[6] To presume that Quebec could negotiate its way back to the exact *status quo ante* [previous status quo] is unrealistic. The FTA is not simply an agreement about liberalizing trade by cutting tariffs: it concerns investment, access to energy, safeguards provisions, services and personal mobility, government procurement, subsidies, and dispute resolution mechanisms. These contractual provisions can be more or less advantageous to each party. Since the new tripartite agreement could not possibly be identical to what now exists, negotiations would occur; even if the U.S.A. did not use this occasion to reopen broad sections of the agreement (as it is attempting to do with Canada's cultural exemptions), on the points under discussion Quebec would have to defend its interests where they conflicted with those of the United States (and Canada). Beyond this, any new agreement would expose Quebec's internal policies to the full scrutiny of its partners and to potential discipline: currently, important aspects of the FTA such as competitive access to government procurement do not apply to the provinces, and it is hard to see how the emerging subsidy regime could fully apply to states and provinces.

Other treaties with the United States would also have to be renegotiated. The Americans' primary concerns would be NORAD and NATO, and Quebec's strategic position might lend it some leverage on nonmilitary matters (though this has not helped Canada much, despite the fact that Canada's northern geography is more important strategically than Quebec's). There remains the Defence Production/Defence Sharing (DP/DS) agreements and the Auto Pact, which is currently under scrutiny in the context of the NAFTA talks. It is unlikely that Quebec would have much impact on the Auto Pact (though it could, with the Americans, support the 60 per cent content rules), and any export benefits under DP/DS would be proportional to Quebec's military procurement.

But the really critical regime for Quebec would be the Canada-Quebec agreement which would necessarily result from a formal declaration of independence by Quebec. And this is crucial, despite the increasing North-South linkages of the Quebec economy. In manufacturing, for instance, Quebec produced $61.5 billion in 1984, of which $15.1 billion went to ROC while $12.1 billion was exported. The critical question is what degree of autonomy would Quebec governments have within the new bilateral regime. Or, put more precisely, given the need for harmonization and coordination in order to maintain the economic advantages of the Canadian common market, would Quebec's sovereign government retain autonomy sufficient to implement the distinctive policies which are supposed to produce its long-term higher growth rate?

Of course this would depend on how events unfold, and the level of uncertainty is high. But again, let us assume that a regretful but not resentful ROC holds together, and is determined to manage the huge complex of its mutual affairs with Quebec to its own advantage.

According to the Bélanger-Campeau Commission, the immediate result would be the status quo. Indeed, the very first Act of the Parliament of an independent Quebec would declare that all federal legislation applies to Quebec until it is changed. As for the Canadian common market,

> ...following the accession to sovereignty, some of the main elements of the common market could be preserved by Quebec keeping in force most existing federal legislation and, subsequently, through some degree of harmonization. Competition, financial institutions, and bankruptcy are important examples in this respect.[7]

The report further suggests harmonization with the other provinces in areas under provincial or shared jurisdiction; this could occur in road transportation and, less formally, in taxation, securities and insurance. Other areas of harmonization would include industrial property, copyright and telecommunications.[8]

Beyond this lies the area of currency and monetary policy. This is a complex matter, but all the essential elements of Quebec's dilemma are present. Individuals' desires for security and capital markets' abhorrence of uncertainty suggest that a separate currency would be ill-advised for Quebec. Hence there could be no separate central bank nor an independent macro-policy stance on the monetary and exchange rate fronts. Instead, Quebec would use the Canadian or the U.S. dollar. In this case it would be subject to decisions of central banks (and governments) in which it had no representation. Demands for parity in decision making would simply be refused as not in the interests of ROC. Of course, Quebec dollar holders would account for about one-quarter of Canadian funds in circulation, and the Quebec government could through its fiscal decisions frustrate Bank of Canada policy. This confers some substantial bargaining power on the Quebec authorities. But would it be as great as Quebec's power within the federation?

Quebec's range of autonomy in industrial policy would be limited by its greater transparency under any possible tripartite FTA. A Canada-Quebec agreement would further limit it. The Bélanger-Campeau Commission favoured a common market, and with good reason, as standard trade theory suggests that smaller economies lose more from the imposition of trade barriers. This implies that there must be a common external tariff, and hence a coordinated negotiating position in international trade talks.

But industrial policy and the maintenance of a common market also flow into the social policy field. An important position of the Bélanger-Campeau Commission was to favour labour mobility within the common economic space. And this implies the "transferability of entitlement" to major social programs including unemployment insurance, social assistance, government pension plans, old age security, and health insurance; as well, coordination in the field of immigration would be desirable.[9] With very few exceptions—language, culture, education, tourism, some transportation, policing, some social services, municipal functions, and perhaps the environment—an independent Quebec would be interested in harmonizing its policies with ROC's.

And here is the nub of the problem. Lack of harmonization would entail economic losses caused by barriers within the common market. The costs of such barriers, or of the transactions necessary to overcome them, would fall disproportionately upon Quebeckers. Harmonization on Quebec's terms would allow it to create a policy environment within which could be achieved the potential extra growth envisaged by those who argue for sovereignty on economic grounds. But harmonization would not be on Quebec's terms. A self-interested ROC would have its own agenda and set of preferences about the new bilateral regime.

What would be the bargaining strength of an independent Quebec? In regime theory the answers range across a wide spectrum. On one side, regimes are seen as fundamentally imperialistic, as the stronger powers reap the lion's share of the benefits. The weaker powers face an economic playing field which is tilted against them, but they have little choice except to sign on because the alternative is worse. At the other extreme is the position that small powers can sometimes "free-ride" within regimes, obtaining advantages they would not get otherwise when great powers negotiate mutually beneficial arrangements which extend to all, or as a *hegemon* bears a disproportionate cost of regime maintenance. Neither extreme view applies here (if anywhere): the ROC-Quebec regime is bilateral, and each party has expertise and alternatives. The applicable principle here, and the middle position in general, is that Quebec's bargaining power would be a straightforward function of its economic weight. On particular issues it may enjoy greater leverage based on ROC's dependence on Quebec markets or Quebec inputs, but these should be offset by vulnerability elsewhere. On average, Quebec's negotiating power should reflect its economic might.

Quebec's Advantage in Federation

Quebec's current share of Canadian GDP is about 24 per cent, yet its current bargaining weight within the Canadian federation is substantially greater than this. A recent study of central government deputy ministers shows that, over the past decade, 30 per cent have been francophones.[10] On examining Cabinet representation in all federal governments from 1957 on, we find that the proportion of Quebec ministers has been, in percentage, 17, 31, 31, 38, 40, 44, 17, 31, 28, and 36. The average proportion of Quebeckers holding the key portfolios of Prime Minister, Finance, External Affairs, Industry and Trade, and Treasury Board since 1957 is 30 per cent—again, much greater than Quebec's population or its weight in the economy would dictate.[11]

Of course, these rough data are not conclusive. These individuals may have been Quebeckers of a particular stripe, or they may have become captured by a new ethos when serving in central government institutions. But given these and other indicators, Quebec's negotiating position within Canada about the policies operating in the common economic space has been stronger than it otherwise would be. Moreover, Quebec's presence in the federation as a province undoubtedly retards centralizing tendencies which are much more pronounced in the other provinces, and so it has retained a greater range of matters under sole provincial discretion than would have been the case had all industrial and social policy initiatives to become candidates for harmonization.

All these matters are speculative and debatable, naturally. For example, some people argue that the current regime is economically untenable for both Quebec and ROC, and that Quebec independence would enable ROC to reconstitute itself in a more centralized form, as a true nation which could then undertake the growth-oriented policies feasible in such a unit. Others suggest that a more decentralized federation would benefit all regions, including Quebec.[12] It seems to me, though, that Quebeckers' best strategy is to keep "the knife at English Canada's throat" by participating fully—indeed, more than fully—in governing the federation, while exercising their provincial powers to the fullest and still maintaining the option, or the threat, of exit. Whether through involvement in the federal cabinet or bureaucracy or in inter-provincial negotiations, this strategy maximizes Quebec's ability to extract concessions from ROC—not in the vulgar form of often wasteful expenditures but in the crucial sense of shaping the policy framework within which its economy will function.

If the economic argument for sovereignty does not hold up, it remains to consider the cultural dimension. Globalization is normally considered to be an economic phenomenon, but it involves culture in fundamental ways. Its effects are twofold. On the one hand is the movement towards a homogeneous world culture, where products, modes of life, and symbols and values are shared around the globe, and in which the *lingua franca* is English. This poses a massive challenge to every distinctive culture and to minority languages everywhere. On the other hand, globalization allows such a creation of wealth that people have much more plentiful resources to devote to cultural development and linguistic maintenance, if they choose to do so.

Necessary Concessions

There is no doubt that francophone Quebeckers feel threatened linguistically, and that they are prepared to defend the basis of their national distinctiveness. After the Supreme Court ruled in 1989 on the issue of outdoor signage in Quebec, and just after the Bourassa government announced its intention to override the Charter, a Gallup poll asked a question which posed a rare outright choice to respondents. It was: "What do you think is more important—the rights of English-speaking Quebeckers to have freedom of speech or the rights of French-speaking Quebeckers to preserve their culture?" This forcing item produced a startling split among respondents on linguistic lines. Of those whose mother tongue was English, 72 per cent assigned higher priority to freedom of speech; among francophones, only 15 per cent made this choice while 78 per cent opted for the collective right of preserving their culture.[13]

There is overwhelming support in Quebec for policies that defend a language whose position in North America is fragile (it has been likened to a sugar cube placed beside an urn of coffee). Such cultural defences preserve francophones' national identity, which is the ultimate foundation of any drive towards national self-determination (regions do not pursue independence because they have distinct economies). It was precisely to diffuse Quebec nationalism by encouraging the use of French in Ottawa and throughout Canada that the central government introduced its bilingualism policies. These policies are supported by Quebeckers, but there is no doubt that when national decisions on language policy are seen to pose a threat to French in Quebec they will be rejected. The sense of cultural and linguistic siege remains strong among Quebeckers, and this insecurity will not fade, especially so long as they live within a constitutional language regime dominated by ROC.

In the face of globalization's challenge to cultural distinctiveness, one set of constitutional changes could reassure Quebeckers about the long-term viability of their society. This would be to devolve jurisdiction over language and culture to the provinces. This might best be accomplished by making these areas of concurrent jurisdiction with provincial paramountcy (though creative use of Section 43 of the Charter may be necessary). The point is simply to provide Quebeckers with a fundamental certainty that insofar as their linguistic and cultural future can be controlled at all, they will control it. Implicitly, such a move would also demonstrate Canada's confidence that Quebec will be fair and tolerant towards its minorities (and it seems probable that with control over these areas achieved, Quebec governments could afford to be more liberal in language regulation than they have been).

Most important, meeting Quebeckers' demands for cultural and linguistic security in a globalizing world would undercut support for those economic arguments in favour of sovereignty which are now circulating in Quebec. These arguments point to a strategy which is highly risky. If they prove fallacious, as seems probable, their cost will be great for ordinary Canadians everywhere. Far better for Quebeckers to control the cultural foundations of their distinctiveness, and to use their position in Canada to reshape according to their needs the regimes within which they compete in the global economy.

Notes

[1] Fortin, Pierre, "How Economics is Shaping the Constitutional Debate in Quebec," in Robert Young, ed., *Confederation in Crisis* (Toronto: James Lorimer & Company, 1991), pp. 35-44. One cannot but have considerable sympathy for arguments about the wasteful effects of federal-provincial competition when considering regional development policy in Quebec, much of which can be read as a competition for voters' loyalty, not merely to a government but also to a state and a constitutional regime. Upon the announcement of Ottawa's new department for Quebec regional develop-

ment, for example, one Conservative backbencher was quoted as saying, "Je ne veux plus parler de constitution, je veux parler de construction" [I don't want to talk any more about constitution, I want to talk about construction] (*Le Devoir*, May 29, 1991).

[2] Proulx, Pierre Paul, "L'Évolution de l'Espace Économique du Québec, La Politique Économique Dans un Monde de Nationalismes et d'Interdépendance, et les Relations Québec-Ottawa," in Commission Sur l'Avenir Politique et Constitutionnel du Québec, *Les avis des spécialistes invités à répondre aux huit questions posées par la Commission*, Document de travail, numéro 4 (Québec, 1991), 867-902.

[3] Bellemare, Diane, "Réponses aux Questions Posées par la Commission sur l'Avenir Politique et Constitutionnel du Québec," in Commission Sur l'Avenir Politique et Constitutionnel du Québec, *Les avis des spécialistes invités à répondre aux huit questions posées par la Commission*, Document de travail, numéro 4 (Quebec, 1991), pp. 21-44.

[4] Large transition costs also raise the question of their distribution. If they are not shared, then along with misery comes an erosion of the solidarity which is supposedly conducive to rapid growth; if they are shared, then at the margin the exit option will be chosen by the more dynamic economic agents, especially anglophones and allophones.

[5] Québec, *Report of the Commission on the Political and Constitutional Future of Québec* (Quebec, March, 1991), pp. 55-56.

[6] Ivan Bernier, "Le Maintien de l'Acces aux Marches Exterieurs: Certaines Questions Juridiques Soulevées dans l'Hypothese de la Souveraineté du Québec," in Commission Sur l'Avenir Politique et Constitutionnel du Québec, *Elements d'analyse economique pertinents a la revision du statut politique et constitutionnel du Québec*, Document de travail, numero 1 (Quebec, 1991), p. 14.

[7] *Report of the Commission*, p. 57.

[8] *Ibid.*, pp. 57-58.

[9] *Ibid.*, p. 61. Note that the PQ members of the commission accepted this position:

> Special importance must be given to maintaining and even increasing Canada's economic space and this to promoting a continuation of the free movement of goods, services, people and capital, as well as to maintaining the tariff union. (Bélanger-Campeau Commission, Report, p. 95, 1st Addendum).

[10] Bourgault, Jacques and Dion, Stéphane, *The Changing Profile of Federal Deputy Ministers, 1967-1988* (Ottawa: Canadian Centre for Management Development, 1991).

[11] Normandin, Pierre G., *Canadian Parliamentary Guide* (Ottawa: n.p., various years).

[12] Courchene, Thomas, "Canada at Play: Alternative Constitutional Games", MS, 1991.

[13] Gallup Canada, Inc., *Gallup Report*, January 12, 1989.

Must Canada Join the U.S.?
Can Canada Join the U.S.?

David Frum

A Nightmare Fantasy

THE QUESTION I'VE BEEN ASKED to address is: If things go wrong, if some reasonable constitutional reform accommodation cannot be reached and Quebec does choose to vacate the premises, will Canada vanish past the flashing teeth and down the gaping maw of the United States, that country where 38 per cent of the population is homeless (as one of the questioners suggested)? This is the familiar nightmare-fantasy of Canadian politics. I call it a nightmare because Canadians so obviously regard it as a dreadful prospect. I call it a fantasy because they so lovingly dwell on it.

It is my own view that, were parts of Canada to vanish down that maw, it wouldn't necessarily be such a bad thing. The United States has created an admirable civilization, but it is also a different civilization from the one that obtains here. Since I'm not Jacobin enough to want to eliminate all national distinctions, I think there is some nice advantage served by the continuing existence of Canada as a separate entity.

I want to begin addressing the question—can Canada retain its independence without Quebec—with one caveat. This question, which is so often asked, is based on an extremely unrealistic prospect: that there will be some moment called the separation of Quebec from Canada. I think that it will not be so neat or so clean. If Quebec votes in some P.Q.-sponsored referendum to leave, what we will have to look forward to is another dozen years of constitutional wrangling. The idea that Quebec will leave and the rest of us will be faced with a crisis and that some parts of us or all of us will choose to assimilate to the United States is not a problem for the immediate future.

However, it could be a problem for the more distant future and I think that it deserves some kind of answer. My own answer to the question is that there's no particular necessity for Canada to join the United States. The premise behind the question is that once Quebec goes, some remaining part of the country, or perhaps all of it, will find the situation so insupportable that assimilation with the United States would be preferred. The impression I have, at least about those parts of the country that are most often spoken of as candidates for joining the United States—the Maritimes and British Columbia—is that it is the presence of Quebec in Canada that has bothered them, not its prospective withdrawal. It would seem that there are a lot of people out West who would prefer a Canada in which they had one-third of the votes, rather than a Canada in which they have one-quarter.

I think that this question is misconceived too because it accepts the Trudeau-ite propaganda that what makes Canada a worthwhile place is Quebec. English Canada has accepted this premise, which carries in its tail the barbed insult that there is nothing particularly worthwhile in the association of English Canada—not only nothing worthwhile, but nothing sustainable.

I think that the day after Quebec goes we will discover that Canada remains as attractive a proposition as it was three days before. The idea that Canada, or parts of it, must then break off rests on the vulgar error that contiguity is essential to the survival of a national state—a proposition that I think most Alaskans would reject. This error is as vulgar as the error that prevails both among sovereigntists and Trudeau-ites, which holds that complete sovereignty is essential to a state, and that therefore nations must have states of their own, no matter how small, that those states must possess all the attributes of sovereignty, and that sovereignty cannot be split.

This is not to say that the adhesion of some parts of Canada to the United States won't happen, only that there is no necessity for it to happen. But I also believe that there isn't much probability that it will happen. It is hard to see the Maritimes volunteering to surrender their subsidies from the rest of Canada, good for them as that prospect might otherwise be. I think it is peculiar that those parts of the country most often spoken of as the likeliest to evacuate Canada—the Maritimes and British Columbia—are the parts of the country that voted most vehemently against the Conservatives in the last federal election, when the Conservatives were campaigning on a platform of closer links with the United States.

There is one final problem: joining the United States is a trickier proposition than most Canadians understand. This goes back to the fantasy part of this national nightmare. I think the relationship that Canada envisages between itself and the United States is that of the nymphette on the cover of vampire books, who is stretching out her white throat in horrified fascination as the spectre comes closer and closer and closer. There is in fact a constituency of precisely one in the United States for absorbing Canada— the half-kooky syndicated columnist Patrick Buchanan who, loud though he may be, is not a very influential person at all.

In order for a territory to adhere to the United States, it has to satisfy a number of criteria that Canada, or any part of Canada, will have difficulty meeting. The first is that the would-be state must be able to convincingly assure the American political system that it will elect a roughly equal number of Republican and Democratic senators. The last time America took on a new territory, you'll notice it took on two states at the same time—Hawaii and Alaska (Hawaii being Republican, and Alaska Democratic).

Canada will also have to assure the American political system that the adhesion of Canada, or parts of Canada, to the United States will not upset the racial balance in the United States. This is an unspoken but important question. Just as Patrick Buchanan favours the absorption of Canada because he wants to increase the number of white people in the United States, so there are powerful constituencies that, for reasons of their own ethnic politics, will want to avoid precisely that.

One more impractical problem remains: working out how Canada will participate in the American political system, a system which has substantially more federal authority than our own and does not offer subsidies to regions (at least, it does not frankly offer subsidies to regions; you have to send your senator to a powerful congressional committee and keep him there, and he has to obtain your subsidies through political manoeuvring). On the other hand, I doubt that medicare will prove to be as much of an obstacle as Canadians often think since I'm very much afraid that, long before Quebec is able to make up its mind whether to go or to stay, there will be national health insurance in the United States. It's a grim private joke of mine that George Bush, when interviewed on leaving office in January of 1997 and asked what the proudest achievement of his presidency has been, will say not the defeat of Iraq but the achievement of national health insurance.

The final difficulty, but not the most complicated is perhaps the most telling, is that Canadians won't make very good Americans. Being an American is a very serious job, while being a Canadian isn't. I don't mean that as a joke. You have to be prepared to get killed for being an American. No one has been killed for being a Canadian in a long time, maybe not ever. You got killed for being an adjunct member of the British Empire, perhaps, but not for being a Canadian. For Americans it's not just that you're at risk every time you fly to Athens; not even that there are 11,000 Soviet nuclear warheads aimed at you. Americans understand that in the last analysis, the security of the whole world rests on them and that explains a great deal of what, to Canadian minds, seems the absurd heights of patriotism of the United States. Canadians don't have that sense of responsibility. They also lack the sense that their country has contributed very much to world civilization. They lack this sense for quite good reasons, because Canada indeed hasn't contributed much towards world civilization while the United States has.

Given that there isn't this necessity, that there isn't much probability, and that even if Canada were to make up its mind to do it, it would encounter immense resistance from the American political system, why do Canadians keep returning to the question of absorption into the United States? It is an obsessively interesting topic for people here and it's something we keep teasing ourselves with, for which I think there are two reasons. First, there is a lot about the American political system and the American way of life that seems to Canadians to be more attractive than their own. America is a society with a higher degree of pride in the existence of the country, a society that seems to deliver more prosperity at less cost in taxes and regulation. We doubt our own capacity to achieve such a society for ourselves unaided, so people in Nova Scotia—like those Pacific islanders who put out landing strips hoping that the great plane will land bringing the consumer goods—think basically that if they fly the American flag, Nova Scotia will be transformed into Cape Cod.

A Probable Outcome

The second, more important reason is that there is now a great hunger in this country for a decisive, once-and-for-all outcome to Canada's constitutional difficulties, whatever that outcome is. The sense I have is that most people would prefer any outcome to talking about constitutional problems for even five more minutes. If there were an independent, French-speaking state in Quebec, and the rest of Canada joined the United States, that would really solve the Canadian question and it would at last be over—the whole Canadian problem would be over. There is a kind of a relief of desperate men that the prospect of absorption therefore evokes. But I'm sorry to say that it seems more probable, for better or for worse, that our constitutional problems will drag on and on and on. We have chosen to go on and on and on with this, and like a protagonist caught in some existential novel of the 1950s, the only thing to do is to accept our fate and bear up under it as stoically as we can.

Separatism and the Quebec Intellectual Tradition

William Johnson

Paradoxes

I'M GOING TO BEGIN BY pointing to some paradoxes. The Quebec population for about a year now has seemed committed to a form of secession called sovereignty, yet this is happening in what is by most objective criteria one of the most successful countries in the world. A United Nations survey in May 1991 put Canada second only to Japan for its social and economic development, rating Canada higher than 158 other countries.

The paradox can be extended. Quebeckers are among the most free, the most prosperous, and the most culturally endowed people on the face of the earth. They have a provincial government with wide powers (in the areas of education and health particularly) which is close to the citizen. And yet the Quebec government is committed to holding a referendum on sovereignty next year.

The paradox of objective criteria is paralleled by attitudes. You might remember that in a *Globe and Mail*-CBC survey of April 1991, a plurality of Quebeckers said they were in favour of sovereignty; and yet 83 per cent of Quebeckers agreed with the following statement: *Canada is the best country in the world to live in.*

The third paradox is that Quebeckers have held an altogether privileged place in the federal political system from which they seem to be alienated. From Confederation in 1867 until 1896, the Conservatives were in power in Ottawa for all but one term, and the foundation of Conservative power was the province of Quebec. Of the 95 years which followed 1896 (when, you remember, Sir Wilfrid Laurier came to power), the Liberals were in power for about 72 of those years, and the basis of their power was Quebec. So Quebec was almost always in the government after Confederation and was the chief basis of the power of the ruling government—and we know in our parliamentary system the enormous difference between being in government (which is total power) and being out of government (which is no power).

Quebec's Intellectual Tradition

In the 95 years since 1896, a Quebecker has been Prime Minister for exactly half the time. Moreover, the present Prime Minister is from Quebec, and the next Prime Minister is almost certainly going to be from Quebec. So there are many paradoxes, and these paradoxes cry out for explanation. My explanation today will not easily appeal to economists or political scientists who would like to be given hard variables. My long experience in observing Quebec has persuaded me that the true explanation of separatism lies in a peculiar *intellectual* tradition in Quebec that portrayed *les Anglais* and the federal government as aliens, as threatening Quebec's most cherished traditions and values, and as a source and cause of all of Quebec's major problems. The solution to Canadian federalism will not be found, I suggest, until this intellectual tradition is confronted on its own terrain, and its xenophobia and irrationality unmasked and made explicit. In other words, Quebec's intellectual tradition must be put on trial, examined, criticized, compared, and de-mythologized. Only when that intellectual tradition has been purged of its anachronistic, hostile, mythologizing anti-intellectual elements will the people of Quebec be able to judge federalism on its merits. Until then the people of Quebec are relying on intellectuals, the eyes and ears of a society, who are blinded and deafened by their own intellectual tradition.

To understand the Quebec intellectual tradition today you have to go back to its origins in the last century, and perhaps a good place to start is Lord Durham's report of 1839. He described French Canadians as "a people with no literature and no history."[1] Much of Quebec's literature and historiography was born precisely as a reply to Durham. No history? François-Xavier Garneau, considered the greatest French-Canadian writer of the 19th century, wrote his three volume *Histoire du Canada* in the decade that followed Durham's report. As historian Pierre Savard notes, "Garneau presented the history of French Canadians as a struggle for survival against the Indians and the Anglo-Americans on the battlefields, and then against the English Canadian oligarchy in the parliamentary arena."[2] Savard also notes that Garneau's reading of French-Canadian history was the dominant interpretation in Quebec's historiography until after the Second World War.

The most influential French Canadian historian of the twentieth century was Lionel Groulx. He also saw French Canadian history as a struggle for survival against *les Anglais*, but pushed it further. In his anthropological views, racial and ethnic groups are meant to be kept separate; when two cultures are mixed by excessive contact or marriage they enfeeble and contaminate each other. Groulx thought that all aspects of English culture must be rejected by French Canada and resisted to the greatest extent possible.

In the period after the Second World War, the dominant school of historiography based at the University of Montreal addressed one question in particular, that of humiliation. Why were French Canadians poorer, less educated, less prominent in industry than English Canadians? And the answer of Guy Frégault, Maurice Séguin, Michel Brunet and others was that the Conquest was the single catastrophe which explained all later history. In a country, even a federal country, where French Canadians are a minority, they will necessarily be poor and oppressed. Their only hope would be in a Quebec government which had to be expanded to the greatest degree possible, while the federal government had to be constrained progressively as much as possible.

More recent historiography, while less overtly ideological or polemical, adds an additional element to the old thesis. It sees Quebec history as having a natural finality, an inherent terminal point of fulfilment, almost an inevitable goal: the independent French state of Quebec (see Paul-André Linteau, Réné Durocher, Jean-Claude Robert and others).

The view of French Canadian history as a secular battle against *les Anglais* and the State of Ottawa has been paralleled in the literature of Quebec for nearly a century and a half. Louis-Honoré Frechette, poet and playwright, was, according to critic David Hayne, the most important man of letters in 19th century Quebec.[3] His principal collection of poetry, *La Légende d'un Peuple* of 1887, was largely inspired by reading Garneau's *Histoire du Canada* and he saw the same enemies—*les Anglais*. Frechette divided French-Canadian history into three periods. The first was the glorious colonization of New France; the second was concerned with the resistance to *les Anglais*; and the third described the persecutions of French Canadians under the British regime. This last period included, at the time of Frechette's writing, the latest outrage—the hanging of Louis Riel, whom he called "the last martyr."

The novel followed the same anti-*anglais* course as poetry. In the 19th century there were two types of novels that were turned out by the dozens. One was the historical novel, the other the *roman du terroir*, celebrating life on the farm. Both types of novels have this in common: they take the *anglais*, or sometimes a native Indian, as the enemy. As critic Roger Le Moine wrote, "These historical novels tell the story of three people: a young man and a young woman who intend to marry, and then a second pretender or aspirant for the hand of the woman, who belongs to an enemy nation, who tries to destroy their plans."[4] The usual subjects of historical novels are the struggles against *les Anglais* and the Americans in New France, the deportation of the Acadians in 1755, and the rebellions of 1837-38. These subjects, of course, keep alive a sense of the *anglais* as the enemy.

The ruralist (*terroir*) novels were much more ideological. They typically present a young man growing up on the farm who is tempted to go to the city or abroad, often because he is fascinated by an alien woman, usually an *anglaise*. But he eventually either mends his ways and comes back to the farm to marry the French-Canadian girl next door or he perishes miserably in the city. The lesson is that French-Canadian virtue flourishes only on the farm. The city is the domain of *les Anglais*, of industry, and of degradation, both moral and national. The literature, in other words, reflected an intelligentsia in opposition to the modern world, to liberalism, protestantism, pluralism, and industrialization. After the French Revolution, French Canada was counter-revolutionary, especially after the failure of the 1837-38 Rebellion. The great reaction set in especially after 1867, when Confederation gave Quebec its own government and thus the opportunity to organize its *very distinct society* in the image of its clericalist elite.

The society was in great tension with its North American surroundings, and the intelligentsia tried to create an insulation against *les Anglais* who were the carriers of all that the official ideology repudiated and resisted. And so, to propagate the counter-revolutionary mentality and the radical conservatism that were officially promoted, literature presented *les Anglais* as people to be shunned; above all, they were *not* to be imitated. On the surface they seemed happier, richer, to have more accessible social mobility, and to lead a less austere and demanding life with fewer children and more possessions. But the novels made it plain that these appearances were really an illusion. *Les Anglais* were really unhappy and shallow, without true religion or true values, without traditions, faith or fatherland. In the words of Maria Chapdelaine, "Around us outsiders came whom we pleased to call barbarians. They have taken almost all power, they have acquired almost all the money. But in the land of Quebec, nothing has changed. Nothing must change."[5]

This passive resistance to *les Anglais* became more active and virulent in the novels that follow the First World War, such as Lionel Groulx's *L'Appel de la Race* (1922) and the great national epic now being made into a film, *Menaud, Maître-Draveur*. Menaud, published in 1937, especially deserves careful study. Menaud is obsessed with driving *les Anglais* out of his mountain. Their very presence is sacrilegious. They have become rich and powerful, but Menaud knows that they are still barbarians. To be employed by them is humiliation or even treason. Menaud considers his own daughter a traitor when she becomes engaged to a Frenchman working as an agent for *les Anglais*. In the novel, *les Anglais* have no names, no faces—they are nothing but an evil and hostile presence.

A sharp break in Quebec's political and social history occurred after the Second World War and during the early 1960s with the Quiet Revolution. The intellectual elite had become disillusioned with the old myths. For a while they decided that they had been misled, that their society had been blocked, and that the values and the institutions of *les Anglais* were more appropriate for a modern society than their own. They rejected agriculturalism and favoured industrialization in the city, and began to reject large families and living for the after-life. They set about changing their institutions, and the keyword that appeared was *rattrapage* (catching up) which acknowledged implicitly that they had been behind, not above, the rest of North America. During this period of grace, some Quebeckers—notably Pierre Juneau, Pierre Trudeau, Gérard Pelletier, and others—set about transforming Canada to meet the demands of French Canadians, especially to have their language and their school rights accepted throughout Canada.

But this small-l liberal period did not last more than a few years. Soon the old stereotypes of *les Anglais* returned under a new, apparently more modern, guise. In the schools the same body of literature, the same corpus of historiography socialized the young students to the same attitudes: the enemy is the *anglais*. Quebec's intellectual class discovered the decoloniza- tion theories of Albert Memmi, Frantz Fanon, Jacque Berque, Jean-Paul Sartre, and it was love at first sight. They rediscovered that *les Anglais* were the oppressors. The source of all the problems of French Canada were not the *québécois*.

In other words, the same old hostile stereotypes could be resurrected under a new guise, the decolonization theory. Poets like Gaston Miron and Paul Chamberland wrote much-admired poems about how they were alienated, dislocated, divided, decomposed, and destroyed in their very being, in their soul, because they were colonized. Instead of singing the glories of French-Canadian farmers, novels now descended into the lower depths of the cities, to discover the horrors caused by colonization. Essays, whole issues of *Liberté* and *Parti pris*, hundreds of articles, dozens of books, explored the new revelation, the new intellectual orthodoxy that the essen- tial state of alienation of Quebeckers is because there is a federal govern- ment and two official languages, and because of the colonizers, *les Anglais*. With the same fervent unanimity as in the past, a torrent of articles and books proclaimed the successor doctrine that Quebeckers can never be truly human, truly integrated, truly mature, happy, prosperous and at peace as long as they are colonized, as long as they are a part of Canada. Jean Bouthillette wrote a much-admired book, *Le Canadien-Français et son Double*, which demonstrated conclusively that French Canadians would always be in a state of degradation until they lived in an independent French state. Degradation was a new theme of literature. It was deemed that portraying degradation was a political act, a form of consciousness raising, and even a first step towards liberation because liberation could only be achieved after a necessary *prise de conscience* [awareness], an explo- ration of the essential degradation which goes with being colonized as part of Canada.

So we came full circle. During *la grande Noirceur* [the great darkness], reality had to be ignored, twisted, camouflaged and reconstructed to make *les Anglais* the source of all poverty and ignorance, thus saving a sacred society from internal criticism and reform. In the new regime, some of the same ultraconservative, reactionary, xenophobic views have returned under a thin ideological disguise, and again reality has to be sacrificed to preserve the myths of the intellectual tradition. Now we are asked to believe that Quebec is like Algeria or Vietnam, and to believe that French Canadians are the "white niggers of America" as FLQ activist Pierre Vollières put it.

The Vulnerabilities of the Tradition

I have tried to delineate an intellectual tradition of fighting *les Anglais* in French Quebec which, I suggest, is the true basis of separatism in Quebec. It is a tradition rooted in the reaction of an ultraconservative society, rejecting the modern world as represented locally by *les Anglais*. The tradition survived its origins and survived the Quiet Revolution because, having occupied so much of the historiography and literature of Quebec, it socialized the adult generations and continues to socialize the younger generations. The tradition also survived because it found a new ideological justification (colonization theory) to return to the scapegoating of *les Anglais* as the true cause of all the reverses, the poverty, the relatively backward school system and so forth. It also gave writers a convenient genre to raise to epic poetry; it gave orators and budding politicians the opportunity for great political statements evoking the emergence of a new country. In other words, an intelligentsia that had chiefly cultivated myths for a century and a half picked up modified forms of the same myths after the Quiet Revolution. The tradition of mythologizing continued as before.

This Quebec intellectual tradition, however, has its vulnerabilities. One is that it conflicts with the liberal tradition of western culture which finds repugnant such crude scapegoating of one ethnic group. We don't approve of scapegoating Jews, blacks, or Pakistanis. Quebec writers might soon, one hopes, find it embarrassing to hold up *les Anglais* constantly as an object of hatred. In their refusal to recognize *les Anglais* as fellow citizens, as partners in the social, political and economic life of Quebec, as neighbours, friends, and even members of the same family, the Quebec intellectual tradition has still not had its own Quiet Revolution; it still lives in the era of *Maria Chapdelaine*, Lionel Groulx, and *Menaud, Maître-Draveur*. *Les Anglais* are still barbarians to be resisted, rather than fellow citizens of a modern state.

But the intellectual tradition suffers from another vulnerability—it exists in defiance of reality, and reality eventually asserts strongly its own claims. Before the Quiet Revolution, the scapegoating of *les Anglais* had the object of defending the reactionary Catholicism of a stifled society, and was a way of not calling into question archaic values in inappropriate institutions. *Les Anglais* (not the various institutions) were to be blamed for all that was unacceptable. The ideological defense worked for a surprisingly long time, but it began breaking down in the 1940s and was swept away with the Quiet Revolution. The new forms of scapegoating present *les Anglais* as a threat to Quebec's language, to its culture, to its identity, to its soul, and to its very existence, but these constantly repeated things rest on faulty demography and faulty linguistics, on bad sociology, and a grievous abdication of common sense. *Disparaître* [to disappear] is not really what threatens Quebeckers, and having two public languages is not really the equivalent of Emile Nelligan's madness[6]; eventually, no matter how often the two orthodoxies are repeated, reality will break through.

The intellectual tradition is largely divorced from reality, and there is a sense in which everyone is outwardly aware of it, though hardly anyone says so. At the height of *Parti pris* and colonization theory, the only logical conclusion from the writings of the time was that *les Anglais* had to be assassinated as quickly and as massively as possible, and yet no one acted on it—not one *anglais* was assassinated. It was fashionable to play at colonial revolution, but at the first *real* assassination in the real world (i.e. that of Pierre Laporte by the FLQ), public opinion turned 180 degrees.

Conclusions

The recent statement that Quebec must hold a referendum on sovereignty and declare independence one year later is the logical conclusion of the intellectual discourse uttered by writers, poets, and politicians for the past generation. But I don't think independence will happen for the simple reason that in the real circumstances of Canada, it is more attractive for intellectuals to *play* at unilateral declarations of independence than to carry them out and face the *real* consequences. In other words, the intellectual tradition of Quebec has a strong element of mythology which requires each generation to go to war against *les Anglais*, but few really want to win that war decisively, or to see real blood, or a real surrender and departure. That is why I think there seems to have been a change of attitude towards *les Anglais* during the last few months. When it looked as though two-thirds of the people were going to vote for independence, when it looked as though the long struggle of Menaud to drive out *les Anglais* was about to succeed, Menaud sat down and may have had a change of heart—just as his creator, Félix-Antoine Savard, shocked many nationalists by voting no in the 1980 referendum. Menaud now seems to be playing with the idea that there might be room on his mountain for both him and *les Anglais* after all, and perhaps the mountain can even remain a part of Canada as long as it is recognized as distinct.

That is my optimistic scenario for the future, but it is not a full or satisfactory solution. There will be no solution to national unity in Canada until Quebec's intelligentsia comes to terms with its own tradition of scapegoating *les Anglais*. In that respect, Quebec's intelligentsia still has not, as a whole, reached the mature discourse one expects of a liberal state at the end of the twentieth century. The ghost of Menaud has yet to be exorcised from Quebec's collective psyche.

Notes

[1] *Report on the Affairs of British North America From the Earl of Durham, Her Majesty's High Commissioner*, Montreal, The Morning Courier, 1839, p. 112.

[2] Pierre Savard, "Garneau, François-Xavier," in *Canadian Encyclopedia*, Second Edition, Volume II, Edmonton, Hurtig, 1988, p. 874.

[3] David M. Hayne, "Fréchette, Louis-Honoré," in *Canadian Encyclopedia, op. cit.* Volume II, p. 842.

[4] Roger Le Moine, "Jacques et Marie, Souvenirs d'un peuple dispersé, roman de Napoléon Bourassa," in Maurice Lemire, éditeur, *Dictionnaire des oeuvres littéraires du Québec,* Tome premier, 2e édition, Montréal, Fides, 1980, p. 403.

[5] Louis Hémon, *Maria Chapdelaine*, Montréal, Fides, 1924, p. 187.

[6] Émile Nelligan, the great French Canadian poet, had an Irish-born father and a French-speaking mother. He became mentally ill and, from the age of 19, spent the rest of his life in a mental hospital. In the 1990 opera *Nelligan,* based loosely on the poet's life, librettist Michel Tremblay suggests that Nelligan's divided personality came from his unnatural state of having parents of different tongues.

Secession or Reform?
Mechanisms and Directions of
Constitutional Change in Canada

Stephen A. Scott

The Constitutional Crisis

IN THE AFTERMATH OF THE Meech Lake debacle, Canada faces a genuine—though in my view, unnecessary—constitutional crisis. At its root is a lack of consensus, a lack of skill and leadership in bringing it about, and, even worse, professional incompetence and political irresponsibility which first contrived a bungled reform proposal and then amplified it into a national trauma.

From this emerge broad questions as to the fate of the Canadian federation. Is the federation to be dismembered, either through lawful means (i.e. the constitutional amendment process laid down in Part V of the Constitution Act, 1982) or by revolutionary means? Or is less drastic constitutional reform to take place through these amendment mechanisms—and if so, what sort of reform is possible and desirable?

In a short paper,[1] I can only offer the general perspectives of one who believes, first, that balanced measures of reform are (with the exercise of some sobriety and restraint) possible, and second, that Canadian people are fully entitled to—and ought to—protect the territorial integrity of their country.

A word, first, on the possibility of reform.

The most controversial (though not, in my view, the most important) element of the Meech Lake accord[2] was its clumsy and ugly attempt to enact a constitutional interpretation clause articulating our national identity, at least in some of its aspects—notably Quebec's identity as allegedly constituting a distinct society. Much like a regulation about frozen juice, it declared that English-speaking and French-speaking people were "concentrated" here or there. So farcical was this proposed interpretation clause that it had to be controlled by yet another clause sharply circumscribing its permissible scope. Hence today's challenge: Can we do better? Is it *possible* to frame such a clause, in *balanced* terms and in untortured English and French, to reflect Canada's various constitutional values and objectives? I think that it is, and by way of example I append my own suggested text (which abandons, as unattainable, the elegant brevity of the American Founding Fathers).

I would emphasize that in my view the failure of Meech Lake is

- not the failure of the Canadian federalism in general
- not the failure of the constitutional amendment processes
- not the failure of Canadian federalism, in the specific sense of its inability to address Quebec's five stated concerns which (with Senate reform) were the subject of the Meech Lake proposals.

Rather, the failure of Meech Lake is, first, the failure of the *substance of a particular proposal* for reform, for a variety of reasons, some legitimate, some not; and second, the failure of the *methods by which this reform was devised*. I refer, in particular, to the denial (which I myself felt keenly) of any opportunity for members of the public to comment on and influence the text of the 1987 Accord *before* its signature. This secrecy put a premium on the ability of the 11 governments around the table—and their delegates and their advisers—to (1) foresee and meet adequately any problems with the substance of the reforms, and (2) more broadly, to represent adequately the various interests not effectively present at the table (aboriginal peoples, linguistic minorities, and so on). Given the secrecy of the process, this would have called for almost superhuman qualities of foresight and skill. These were not forthcoming. A huge gamble was taken and lost.

I believe that a more open process could have accommodated Quebec's concerns. Moreover, I am morally certain that a more open process in 1987 would have prevented signature of an Accord which could not, in the end, be implemented, and which made matters far worse than if it had never been signed at all. It must now be the task of all who are in positions of leadership within Canadian society to prove that our federalism can indeed meet a wider range of legitimate concerns of *all* Canadians, including Quebeckers.

Thirdly, the failure of the Meech Lake Accord is, even more than a failure either of its substance, or of the methods of its genesis, a failure also of the extreme methods employed in the attempt to secure its passage. The 11 governments signatory to the 1987 Accord could not and did not purport to promise that the houses of Parliament, or the provincial legislative assemblies, would pass the Constitution Amendment, 1987.[3] They promised only to submit it to them. The agreement said this:

> The Prime Minister of Canada will lay or cause to be laid before the Senate and House of Commons, and the first ministers of the provinces will lay or cause to be laid before their legislative assemblies, as soon as possible, a resolution, in the form appended hereto, to authorize a proclamation to be issued by the Governor-General under the Great Seal of Canada to amend the Constitution of Canada.

Yet, in the three years that the Meech Lake amendment was before the public and treated as open for enactment (which, in my view it still is, without any time limit) it was repeatedly asserted that the 1987 Accord had promised to Quebec the enactment of its proposals. If these proposals were not enacted (we were warned) there would be a breach by Canada of a promise to Quebec. This was repeated by many proponents of Meech Lake, including federal and provincial Ministers of the Crown, such as The Honourable Lucien Bouchard. In effect, then, *the constitutional amendment process was treated as a rubber stamp to implement First Ministers' decisions, and when it did not work in this way, the political consequences were severe.*

Governments must approach with special sensitivity the use of constitutional amendment processes. Obviously these mechanisms do operate in the context of responsible parliamentary government, a system in which ministries are normally able to secure passage of their measures through the houses to which they are responsible. However this *should* not and *need* not mean that it is acceptable for ministries to *force* or to *try* to force constitutional amendments through their parliamentary processes. Constitutional amendments are usually too important and virtually irrevocable. Still less should ministries make—or even appear to make—or let themselves *be* represented as making—intergovernmental or other public commitments to force passage as a matter of the confidence of the House.

Moreover, even within the framework of responsible parliamentary government, a ministry's political undertaking is no better than its tenure of office. Ministries and ministers come and go, and so do members of parliament and of legislatures. It is even more preposterous, and more dangerous, to argue that one government's political commitments bind *later* ministries and legislative bodies in their judgments on constitutional amendments.

All of this is to say what should be obvious: the constitutional amendment processes—whatever they are—should be respected and not abused. In my view, they were not respected in the attempts to secure passage of the Constitution Amendment, 1987. Apart from the myth that Quebec had been promised its enactment, there was the further and even more dangerous myth that the 1982 constitutional reforms had represented an outrage upon Quebec for which the rest of Canada, to use The Honourable Lucien Bouchard's term, must "atone." From June 1987 onward, this atrocious myth was given currency by the Prime Minister of Canada and the Premier of Quebec among others, obviously because it created pressure to pass the Meech Lake amendment. In the interests of the historical record, I would simply point out:

1. The 1982 reform was an overwhelming success for the "common front" of eight provinces (*including* Quebec), which obtained, most notably:
   a. an amending formula which was their own proposal with relatively limited modifications, and
   b. an override clause allowing a legislature to free itself from most of the limits imposed by the Canadian Charter of Rights and Freedoms.
2. The Quebec government itself, in the end, objected to only *three* aspects of the 1982 reforms. This was explicitly and publicly stated by Premier Lévesque.
3. The Quebec Liberal opposition in the National Assembly took the position in 1981 that the Parti Québécois government was seeking to prevent a settlement with the government of Canada by *escalating its demands in course of negotiation*. Failure was thus laid at the door of the then Quebec ministry, not on any betrayal or bad faith by the federal government or other provinces. This can be seen in

black and white in the Debates of the National Assembly of Quebec, and I have documented these events in my published paper written for the Macdonald Commission.[4]

For three years these myths—the alleged outrage of 1982 and the alleged promise of ratification of Meech Lake—were propagated assiduously. Meech Lake (it was said) was the "last chance" for Confederation. Rejection of Meech Lake would be a repudiation and rejection of Quebec. It is scarcely surprising, then, that as in a Greek tragedy the principal figures in the Meech Lake drama have brought about the very result they sought to avoid. Though I opposed Meech Lake, I accept the legitimacy of the five concerns which Quebec advanced at the outset of the negotiations and believe they always were, and still are, capable of accommodation by balanced measures of reform. I think it would still be useful to prove this to Quebec. If these five were foremost in 1987, are they of no significance now?

Secession

What then of the secession of Quebec? Clearly, this can be accomplished in only two possible ways: (1) in accordance with Canadian law, that is, under the constitutional amendment procedures, or (2) against Canadian law, in other words, by revolutionary action.

I realize that I am breaking a taboo and articulating positions which are anathema to many in Quebec, not all of them strong French Canadian nationalists. However, if we negotiate constitutional change on the premise that Quebec may secede at will, we risk dismantling the federation in order to save it. The premises of a negotiation are usually crucial to its outcome. The federation must not deliberate and negotiate in a drugged state and with its hands tied behind its back, nor under deadlines and threats of secession imposed by the Quebec government.

A. *Change by Lawful Means*

We cannot today tarry on the esoteric, though important, questions as to which or what combination of the amendment procedures in Part V of the Constitution Act may or must be employed to give Quebec independence by lawful means. The relevant constitutional changes would necessitate recourse to one or more of the bilateral and multilateral mechanisms of

Part V. Amendments can be initiated by resolution of the National Assembly of Quebec. All relevant procedures require the authorization of both houses of the federal Parliament, or at least the consent of the House of Commons, if after a 180-day delay the Senate will not concur (Section 47). There can thus be no lawful secession without the consent of the House of Commons of Canada. In addition, the legislative assemblies of a certain number of provinces must also authorize the relevant amendments: perhaps all provinces (Section 41); perhaps two-thirds (Sections 38 and 42); conceivably Quebec alone (Section 43).

The federal House of Commons, representing the Canadian people as a whole, can (and in my view should) make it clear that it will not authorize the secession of any province under any circumstances, or at any rate not unless the people of Canada as a whole have clearly and deliberately agreed to both the principle and the terms of separation, as for example by a sufficiently large majority in a referendum.

B. *Change by Revolutionary Means*

Unilateral declaration of independence by Quebec—that is, revolutionary change—is sometimes suggested within Quebec as a possibility if Canada as a whole will not accede to an expressed wish by the people of Quebec to achieve independence. Pursuit of Quebec independence, especially by unlawful means, raises the major question as to how the people of Quebec are to manifest their will: indirectly through legislative institutions, or directly by referendum—and in either instance by what majority? Would the courts rally to a unilateral declaration of independence (UDI)? Would they be purged if they did not?

Rebellion would scarcely serve Quebec's best interests. Moreover, Canada retains and ought to exercise its legitimate right of self-defence to repel insurrectionary acts just as Quebec (I believe) would clearly do in response to threats to its own territorial integrity after independence. I do not think that a revolutionary government in Quebec, as opposed to the government of Canada, would be in any position to control most of the land-mass of the province, particularly the sparsely-populated northern half of the province that is inhabited largely by aboriginal Canadians. And it is in the interest of Quebec society as a whole to keep order in urban areas. We should not, in sum, be intimidated by threats of UDI.

C. *Principles Governing Canadian Sovereignty and Territorial Integrity*

It may be helpful if I present my thoughts on these issues as a series of propositions:

1. *Canada: the sovereign state and its people.* Canada, as an integral whole, is a sovereign state, every part of which belongs to *all* of its people so far as political sovereignty is concerned.

2. *No double standard on indivisibility.* There can be no double standard on the issue of divisibility. Any principle which argues that Quebec is indivisible makes Canada equally indivisible. And any principle which argues that Canada is divisible makes Quebec equally divisible.

3. *The constitution: sole source of authority.* Canada's sovereign powers are exercised by its people through federal and provincial institutions, whose very existence and powers are established and defined by the constitution, and by the constitution alone.

4. *The provinces: creatures of the constitution.* Canadian provinces, as much as the federation itself, therefore depend completely upon the constitution for their rights and powers, and even their existence. Provinces can make no valid claim to any rights beyond, or outside, the constitution. The provinces are not—either legally or historically—"prior to" Canada, nor are they the "creators of" Canada: the law rather creates both.

5. *The constitutional amendment processes: sole means of change.* There is no legal basis for any constitutional change—and therefore no right of secession by any province, territory, or other political subdivision of Canada—except through the means of change provided by the constitution itself. (As Lincoln said, "The States have their status in the Union, and they have no other legal status. If they break from this they can only do so against law and by revolution.")[5]

6. *Boundary lines mean nothing by themselves.* A line drawn as a boundary has no legal meaning—nor, indeed, any moral or other meaning—beyond its actual purpose. A line defining the boundaries of a province, municipality, or other political unit exists for no purpose other than the exercise of whatever powers are conferred upon it by law from time to time. A political boundary does not, merely because it exists, define a potential sovereign state.

7. *Rights of the people of a province: simply to govern a province.* In particular, the people of a province, and their political institutions, have no legal right, nor for that matter any plausible moral or other right, to govern its territory otherwise than as a province of Canada and within the constitution of Canada. A province is what it is, no more, no less.

8. *A boundary does not create a right to sovereignty.* The existence of a provincial, municipal, or other boundary creates, in itself, no basis whatsoever for a claim of entitlement to sovereignty by the inhabitants of the territory. They cannot plausibly claim "to pull themselves up by their bootstraps" to a higher status. Any aspiration to greater powers or higher status depends on the will of the country as a whole.

9. *Dismemberment of the federation depends on the will of the whole Canadian people, as do boundaries of a new state.* Since the dismemberment of the federation depends on the will of the Canadian people as a whole, as exercised through their constitutional amendment procedures, there is no reason why the Canadian people are obliged to consent to the secession of any province; or, if they do consent, to allow it to secede with its existing boundaries or any other particular boundaries.

10. *An independent Quebec has no valid historical or legal claim to the northern part of the present province.* The immense territories added to Quebec by the Canadian Parliament in 1898 and 1912 were territories under English (and later British) sovereignty long before the cession of New France in 1763, and had no connection with New France. These territories were added to Quebec to be governed as part of a Canadian province. It is sheer effrontery to demand that the 1898 and 1912 territories should form part of an independent Quebec. Without these territories it is highly doubtful that Quebec would be economically viable as a sovereign state—at any rate, viable at a level acceptable to its people.

11. *Duty of the Parliament and government of Canada: defence of the constitution, laws, and territorial integrity of Canada.* It is the duty of the Parliament and government of Canada to enforce and defend the constitution and laws—and therefore the territorial integrity—of Canada against its enemies, whether foreign or domestic. This is obviously so in the everyday case of law enforcement against common criminals. The duty to defend the constitution, laws, and territory against foreign invaders is also self-evident. It is equally so as regards rebels attempting the overthrow of the Canadian state

in all, or part, of Canada's territory. A unilateral declaration of independence by members of the legislature of a province or by anyone else, with or without a referendum, is an act of, or invitation to, treason, and the treason is complete when force is used to carry out the purpose of overthrowing the government. Under Canadian law, in sum, an attempt to overthrow the government is criminal as well as invalid.

12. *Use of force in defence of the constitution: legitimate self-defence.* The use of force to defend the constitution, laws, and territorial integrity of Canada is simply legitimate self-defence. The odium of resort to force properly lies on those who attack the constitution, laws, and territory of Canada, and not upon those who defend the *status quo*. The *status quo* represents the rights both of the Canadian people as a whole, and also of every individual Canadian who wishes to keep the country as one.

13. *Use of force in northern Quebec.* Even if, in face of a unilateral declaration of independence within Quebec, the Canadian people or their parliament and government decided not to exercise their right to defend all of the territory of Quebec by force, the use of the limited amount of force needed to retain the sparsely-inhabited territories of northern Quebec would probably be effective to frustrate any attempt by Quebec to secede, with or without the northern portion of the province. As an absolute minimum, it could be made perfectly clear that this will be done.

14. *Right of "self-determination."* It is difficult to discern any consensus at all as to the conditions of an internationally recognized right of self-determination, who enjoys it, when and how it may be exercised, and what territory it applies to. It cannot plausibly be a right to assert repeated fresh claims, each of which would bring the state to an end at any time. Positive international law seems clearly to attribute the right of self-determination only to Canada as a whole, and not to any territorial subdivision or minority. It seems preposterous to assert that Canada can be brought to an end at any time at the demand of one of its provinces. So far as Quebec is concerned, the population of Quebec, through its elected representatives or its voters, opted for Canada in 1867 and again in 1980. I would argue that the issue of self-determination, if it existed, is closed; the people—and province—of Quebec remain free, like all others, to seek constitutional change *within* the Federation *by constitutional processes.* Assuming, however, that the French-Canadian people within Quebec, as a group, have a moral right of self-determination or one based in international law, so do others in the

province: aboriginal peoples, for example, and other non-French Canadians. And any right of French Canadians to self-determination can extend only over a limited portion of the present territory of Quebec.

15. *Partition of Quebec.* Demands for the independence of Quebec thus compel consideration of *partition* of the province. In the event that Quebec seeks and Canada permits the independence of Quebec, new provinces of Canada could and should be established, or a rump province retained, both in what is now northern Quebec, and also in those portions of southern Quebec remaining loyal to Canada.

16. *Bargaining on reform.* Bargaining on constitutional reform must not take place on the basis that Quebec can secede if it is dissatisfied with the progress or with the results. Rather it should be based on the principle that all legitimate concerns of Quebeckers, and of other Canadians, can be accommodated by balanced measures of reform.

Notes

[1] Excerpts from this paper have been published in The *Financial Post*, June 15-17, 1991, and in *The Gazette*, Montreal, Tuesday, June 18, 1991. Discussion may be found in the following press items: Clyde H. Farnsworth, "Symposium Tallies Cost of Quebec Separation," *New York Times*, Thursday, June 6, 1991, p. A7, also published under the title "Experts Say a Free Quebec Could Cope" in *International Herald Tribune*, Friday, June 7, 1991, p. 3; Marcel Adam, "Tout le Canada devrait se prononcer sur le projet de séparation du Québec," *La Presse*, Montreal, June 4, 1991; "Un Américain s'étonne qu'après 20 ans on s'interroge sur le droit de sécession," *La Presse*, Montreal, June 11, 1991; Michel C. Auger, "Partition ou Guerre Civile," *Le Journal de Montréal*, Montreal, June 20, 1991, p. 26; William Johnson, "Right to Secede is not Clear-cut," *The Gazette*, Montreal, Friday, May 31, 1991, p. B-3; editorial, "'Reality Shower' hits sovereignists," *The Montreal Downtowner*, Montreal, June 19, 1991, p. 4. On reactions within the Quebec Government, see Stéphane Bureau "Les frontières d'un Québec indépendant font la manchette aux États-Unis," *La Presse*, Montreal, June 8, 1991, p. F7.

[2] Signed at Ottawa, June 3, 1987, by the Prime Minister of Canada and the first ministers of all the provinces. Its text is most widely available in a

publication entitled *A Guide to the Meech Lake Constitutional Accord* (Government of Canada, Ottawa, August 1987), and the French version in the companion publication *Guide de l'Accord Constitutionnel du Lac Meech* (Gouvernement du Canada, août 1987).

[3] The *Constitution Amendment, 1987* is the *Schedule* to the *Motion for a Resolution to Authorize an Amendment to the Constitution of Canada* which itself was appended to the *1987 Constitutional Accord* (*supra*, n. 2). Clause 1 of the *Accord*, quoted in the text, is in substance an agreement as to steps to be taken towards enactment of the *Constitution Amendment, 1987*. The amendment was never enacted for want of authorizing resolutions from the legislative assemblies of Manitoba and Newfoundland. For practical purposes, therefore, the *Constitution Amendment, 1987* can be taken as synonymous with the "Meech Lake" proposals.

[4] "The Canadian Constitutional Amendment Process: Mechanisms and Prospects," in Beckton and Mackay, eds., *Recurring Issues in Canadian Federalism* (Ottawa, 1986), pp. 77ff.; the publication is Vol. 57 of the Royal Commission's published studies. The French version is *Les Dossiers permanents du fédéralisme canadien*; see pp. 81ff.; this may be referred to for the original French-language texts of the passages translated into English in *Recurring Issues*. The historical account is found in the concluding portion of the paper; in the English version see "Quebec and the Amending Process," pp. 94-105; in the French version, "Le Québec et le processus de modification de la Constitution," pp. 99-111. Here, in my translation, are particularly forceful remarks of a Liberal member who later held various senior portfolios in Robert Bourassa's government. M. Michel Gratton, *Journaux des Débats de l'Assemblée nationale du Québec*, 3rd Session, 32nd Legislature, pp. 415-16 (November 25, 1981):

> I say, Mr. President, very clearly, without ambiguity, that the motion which we are debating today is part of this strategy. The strategy requires that the Government never sign any agreement, an agreement which would oblige it to accept a new Canadian constitution which would apply to Quebec, because that would automatically say that it accepted that Quebec has its place within Canada, hence there is no reason to wish to bring about independence. I said last week, Mr. President, that the best way never to sign any agreement, is still to refuse to negotiate, as the Government has done. That's why we are being spoken to about this motion which, according to the Prime Minister [i.e., Premier René Lévesque], once again yesterday, is the vital minimum that Quebec

can accept. What is curious, Mr. President, is that, on November 5, at the end of the constitutional conference at Ottawa, the Prime Minister identified three subjects which prevented him from granting his support and signing the agreement: the question of access to school in the language of the minority; the question of financial compensation in cases of opting out; and the question of mobility.

How is it that, if there were three subjects on November 5, we now find 15 in the Prime Minister's motion? It's the leader of the Opposition who established it clearly yesterday. There were three of them on November 5, and, all of a sudden, there are 15. It is easy enough to understand...How is the Prime Minister trying to redeem himself? By presenting his motion which he has deliberately drafted in such a way as to force the federal government, to invite the federal government, to proceed without Quebec's consent; because, then, he will be able to play the offended virgin, to cry rape, and what else besides? He will try to inflame passions, by appealing to nationalism, because it is known that this works.

References in the quoted passage to the "President" are references to the President of the National Assembly of Quebec—in other words, the Speaker of the province's legislative assembly. References to the "Prime Minister" are references to the Premier of Quebec, Hon. René Lévesque. (For similar observations by M. Claude Ryan and other members, see the references given in my notes.)

5 John G. Nicolay and John Hay, eds., *Complete Works of Abraham Lincoln,* 12 vols. (New York, The Tandy Thomas Company, 1894), Vol. VI, p. 315. The quoted passage appears in a remarkable "Message to Congress in Special Session", July 4, 1861, at VI, p. 297 ff.

PROJET D'UN
NOUVEL ARTICLE 2 DE LA LOI
CONSTITUTIONNELLE DE 1867

(18 décembre 1990)

2. La fédération canadienne affirme:

(i) vouloir assurer, dans le respect de la primauté du droit, à tout son peuple héritier et gardien des diverses cultures de nombreuses origines, les avantages de la liberté, de l'égalité des chances et du bien-être économique;

(ii) assumer une responsabilité particulière envers ses peuples autochtones et reconnaître leur statut de premières nations du Canada;

(iii) reconnaître que le Canada repose non seulement sur les intérêts communs à tout son peuple, et leur poursuite au moyen des institutions de la fédération, mais aussi sur l'identité propre de chacune de ses provinces et chacun des ses territoires;

(iv) vouloir assurer la survivance et la vigueur, partout au Canada, de ses deux langues officielles, le français et l'anglais;

(v) reconnaître que le Québec, unique par sa majorité francophone et sa société distinctive, est garant de la survivance et de la vigueur de la langue française au Canada;

(vi) reconnaître que la langue et la culture distinctive françaises sont à la fois une ressource et un patrimoine, et vouloir assurer leur survivance et leur vigueur non seulement au Québec, leur principal foyer historique, mais partout dans la fédération;

(vii) reconnaître que le Parlement du Canada et les législatures des provinces peuvent, d'une manière conforme aux principes des sociétés libres et démocratiques, exercer leurs pouvoirs afin de préserver et de promouvoir, dans la mesure qui leur revient, ces attributs et ces objets de la fédération, et tout spécialement, dans le cas de la législature du Québec, afin de préserver et de promouvoir sa langue et sa culture de prédominance française;

et la Constitution du Canada sera ainsi interprétée.

DRAFT OF A PROPOSAL FOR A
NEW SECTION 2 OF THE
CONSTITUTION ACTS, 1867

(December 18th, 1990)

2. The Canadian federation affirms:

(i) its resolve to secure, under the rule of law, the advantages of liberty, equal opportunity, and economic well-being, to all its people, inheritors and bearers of the diverse cultures of many lands;

(ii) its special responsibility to its aboriginal peoples, and their standing as the first nations of Canada;

(iii) its recognition that Canada is founded, not only upon the common interests of all of its people and their pursuit through the institutions of the federation, but also upon the individual identity of each of its provinces and territories;

(iv) its resolve to ensure the survival and vigour, throughout Canada, of its two official languages, English and French;

(v) its recognition that Quebec, unique in its French-speaking majority and in its distinctive society, is a guarantor of the survival and vigour of the French language in Canada;

(vi) its recognition that the French language and distinctive culture are at once a resource and a heritage, and its resolve to ensure their survival and vigour not only within Quebec, their principal historic home, but throughout the federation; and

(vii) its recognition that the Parliament of Canada and the legislatures of the provinces may, in a manner consistent with the principles of free and democratic societies, exercise their powers in order to preserve and promote these attributes and objects of the federation, so far as they pertain to each; and more especially, in the case of the legislature of Quebec, in order to preserve and promote its predominantly French linguistic character and culture;

and the Constitution of Canada shall be interpreted accordingly.

On the Economic Consequences of Quebec Separation

John McCallum

THERE IS A QUESTION AS to whether "change theorists" in economics have much to contribute to this debate on federalism. I'm not sure whether they do, at least in the sense of trying to help one or another side "win" the debate. My role is to be perfectly neutral. I will speak therefore of the economic *consequences* of Quebec separation, rather than the economic *costs*.

Costs of Separation

My first point on this topic of economic consequences concerns what you might call credibility of communication. I think the average Quebecker takes poorly to statements coming from Toronto that Quebec separation will produce dire economic consequences, and reacts badly even to such statements coming from McGill. So I hope that what I say will be seen to be balanced.

The other initial point that is extremely important is that the costs of separation are not just costs to Quebec. I think that these costs would also be quite substantial to the rest of Canada.

The third preliminary point is the question of whether the breakup would be harmonious or acrimonious. Economists don't really have much to say about this. If we appeal to history, then I think we would come down on the side of acrimony. If we say that history is irrelevant, as many people often do in the present context, then we have no precedents. So most of what I say is based on the assumption of a relatively harmonious breakup in which the two parties or several parties try to do things in a rational, calm fashion. Consequences would be worse than anticipated—how much worse I don't know—if the case became highly acrimonious.

As for legal discontinuity, there exists a fascinating document, particularly if you are not a lawyer but are used to reading such documents. It is a speculative discussion in the Bélanger-Campeau report by José Woehrling,[1] which sets out in detail the various steps and procedures that would have to be taken for Quebec to separate, along two possible tracks; first, Quebec separating with Canada's agreement—that is, constitutionally and by Canadian rules—and second, without Canada's agreement. It's very interesting to set those things out in detail and then have economists, lawyers and historians respond as to how they think it would work in practice. One study in progress is going to argue that what we have now in the Canadian economic union is a web of extremely complex regulations, rules and laws that somehow make the system work. If you try to take that system apart and put it back together, it's not going to be easy.

A related point made by Tom Courchene is if you take apart the Canadian economic union and put it back together again (and even if you can't put it back together again), you'd be substituting a legal binding kind of arrangement, like the Free Trade Agreement, for something which is held together by top political deals and constitutions. The legal constraints under an economic union are, in fact, much more binding and the result is essentially less real sovereignty to the constituent members when the rules are constitutional/political rather than legal. So on dividing the deck after the breakup, I think there are three questions to ask. The first is what would be Quebec's share of debts and assets?

Quebec's Share

The figures I have seen range from about one-sixth, which is the Bélanger-Campeau view, to one-third, which is the view I heard in Western Canada. In the West they are of the opinion that Quebec's share of the debt would depend on the fiscal balances at the time; since Alberta is not a contributor, Alberta's share of the debt if Canada broke up would be negative while that of Quebec and other seceding provinces would be correspondingly higher. Economists were kind enough to accept a zero share rather than a negative share but according to their calculations, Quebec's share would be one-third. So we have figures from one-sixth to one-third, of which the average happens to be one-fourth—Quebec's share of the population.

I think the second question is, in a way, more interesting and possibly more difficult: in the event of separation, *how* would this debt be transferred? At one extreme, one can imagine that what remains of Canada would reclaim the full legal liability for 100 per cent of the debt. However, if Quebec would promise to make payments to Canada (which, according to some lawyers, is the legal situation), the seceded state would not have liability for the debt. At the other extreme, Quebec would quickly have to take on a debt corresponding to whatever its share was. What would be the mechanics of effecting that transfer, and the reaction of money markets? This is indeed a complex issue which we would want to investigate and to which I don't really have the answers at this moment. But it clearly would not be easy.

Canada's Share

Separation would be even more difficult if the departure of Quebec from Canada provoked some further breakup of the country. If the legal argument is correct, Quebec's departure would be an incentive for other provinces or regions to leave. If it is only the part that remains which bears legal liability for the debt, the stakes are extremely high and there is an immense scope for strategic behaviour. One of my colleagues at McGill has the theory that Confederation only came together because of debt—public debt—and that Confederation is likely to prevail for that same reason. So that's the second issue.

Monetary Policy

The third question involves money and exchange rates, and here I think that even though there has been a lot of discussion about this at certain times, it is really rather simple. Virtually everyone in Quebec who has commented on this assumes that if Quebec does separate it would continue to use the Canadian dollar for at least five to ten years. Once things get stabilized there may be a Quebec currency, but I don't think anyone in Quebec is contemplating the idea of issuing a new Quebec currency at the moment of independence. Moreover, I've heard discussions on this point in various places, and I can't see any way in which the rest of Canada could stop Quebec from using the Canadian dollar if it so chose. The rest of Canada probably wouldn't try, but even if it did I don't think it would succeed. If that is the case it seems to me pretty clear that Quebec would continue to exist in a monetary union, whether it was *de jure* or *de facto*. I don't think we'd have other currencies floating around.

Quebec, in this case, would lose control over Canadian monetary policy and maybe even lose basic revenue, although that could be negotiated in the context of the debt allocation. There may be debate on flexible exchanges, but that is something we always debate anyway, so I think Quebec would keep using Canadian dollars. At the moment of greatest instability—that is, separation—I think there would be extraordinary concern and capital flight from the province of Quebec. That is precisely why I think separation won't happen.

Impact on Trade

Finally, I think trade related issues are contentious. Some of the most authoritative people from Quebec and the rest of Canada are writing on these issues.

There are questions regarding textiles, clothing, milk, and turkeys. For instance, Quebec is a major producer of textiles and clothing. Would the rest of Canada cut its tariffs and quotas on these products? Quebec produces something like 48 per cent of the milk quotas for Canada, so what would happen there? It's interesting to note the findings of Bélanger-Campeau in this regard. When Quebec was deciding which assets it would keep its share in, it didn't want to keep very many crown corporations, but one asset that it would retain was its share of the Canadian Dairy Commission. I think that there would be discussion on that, and there are legal questions as to what the rest of Canada could or could not do with regard to these milk quotas.

Nor is it just a question of Quebec-dominated industries; there is also the question of what is going to happen to the Auto Pact. Ontario is more dependent upon the Auto Pact than is Quebec, and it seems very likely that, at a minimum, the Auto Pact would have to be renegotiated, because the Americans would not be terribly happy with it in the event of Quebec separating.

And what about the Free Trade Agreement? It clearly would have to be renegotiated since, in moving from two countries to three, Quebec and Canada could potentially act in concert, which the Americans probably wouldn't like. The question is what would the United States do, and especially what would the business lobby groups do? The U.S. government might want to act in the most peaceful fashion, but the business lobby groups would see a chance to turn things to their advantage. And what would the rest of Canada do when the majority didn't want free trade in the first place? By the time of separation there might be three N.D.P. governments hostile to free trade at the provincial level, making up two-thirds or three-fourths of the population of Canada outside Quebec.

Notes

[1] José Woehrling, "Les Aspects juridiques de la redéfinition du statut politique et constitutionnel du Québec," in *Eléments d'analyse institutionnelle, juridique et demotinguestique pertînents à la revision du statut politique constitutionnel du Québec*, Document de travail, numéro 2, Bélanger-Campeau Commission.

First-Generation Canadians and the Constitutional and Sovereignty Debates

Jagdish Handa

Separation in a World Context

THE CONSTITUTIONAL DEBATE IS ABOUT separation—separation of Canada into two countries, separation of its people into more clearly defined peoples, and of its culture into more clearly defined cultures. First-generation Canadians are perhaps the only Canadians who have already experienced such separations. They may thus have something useful to contribute to the Constitutional debate.

Many, like me, have first-hand knowledge of the independence of their countries as part of the decolonization process. I was in India in 1947 when it separated from Britain and the British Empire, and when it split into India and Pakistan. I was in Kenya in 1963 when it became independent from Britain. These were political and legal separations, I believe for reasons similar to those at play in Quebec in the last decade. In each case there were endless discussions on the economic costs of separation, without much consensus about whether the country would be better off or not given its close economic ties to Britain. Would per capita income go up or down? How would certain assets be divided? There were discussions of legal and historical precedents and of historical boundaries. And, in the final analysis, none of these mattered.

What then did matter to the final decision on whether to separate? Let me express this in the words of Mahatama Gandhi in Attenborough's film "Gandhi." In response to the statement from an assistant to the British

Viceroy of India that "without British administration this country will be reduced to chaos," Gandhi's reply was "You are masters in someone else's home...It is time you left...I beg you to accept that there is no people on earth who would not prefer their own bad government to the good government of an alien power...Like other nations, we will have our own problems. But they will be ours." There is no hint here that economic considerations were being pertinent to the decision. Nor is there of the legal rights of the citizens, nor of historical association nor of historical boundaries. To me the issue is one of feelings, of a gut feeling of who *we* are and that others are different in an essential way, of *us* and *them.*

Us and Them

The concept of *us* and *them* is very apt between the anglophone and the francophone groups in Canada. It underlies Hugh MacLennan's designation of them as the two solitudes. But it also applies to Canada *vis-à-vis* Britain and the U.S.A.

Canada became a British colony by the Treaty of Paris of 1763, and those who dominated the colony called themselves British. But over time they ceased to feel themselves sufficiently British to be content to be ruled by the British Parliament and government. They had to press for their own legislature and eventually for Dominion (in this case a truncated form of independence) status in the Statute of Westminster, 1931. They wanted to be masters in their own house, for the British—no matter how close in culture, language and institutions—had by then become *others.* But the Statute of Westminster was not the final act of the separation of Canada from Britain, for it did leave several residual powers and elements associated with these *others.*

The British Parliament still had the ultimate power to amend the British North America Act of 1867; it could in fact legislate on a regular basis for Canada; its flag was Canada's flag; its anthem was Canada's anthem, and so on. Canada's nationalism *vis-à-vis* the British eventually was to replace these powers and symbols with Canadian ones: its own flag, its own anthem and eventually its own constitution. Each was a landmark on the road to the separation of Canada from Britain. The struggle to patriate the constitution lasted from the 1920s to 1982, when the British parliament gave up its residual powers over Canadian laws. Canada was master in its own house after all, for better or for worse.

A parallel movement to the constitutional separation from Britain was occurring in Quebec. Its inhabitants shared the same land and to an outsider were of the same culture, but they regarded themselves as of two groups, *us* and *them*. The anglophones were not part of the majority culture, could not identify with it and began to feel that, though still in Canada, they were strangers in Quebec. Thus started the slow trek of anglophones out of Quebec that has been a feature of the Quebec countryside and small towns since the 1940s and is now a feature of its metropolis, Montreal. The francophones increasingly defined the culture of the areas outside Montreal, dominated that of Montreal, and increasingly pressed for the patriation to Quebec of various legislative and administrative powers. They have come a long way from the effective division of powers that existed in, say, 1940, but not all the way to becoming masters of their own house. If my thesis is correct, their feeling of *us* and *them* will eventually lead to separation from Canada.

There have been many landmarks along the route to separation. The laws and customs that have emerged in the last few decades on displaying the Quebec flag in public, and on its size relative to the Canadian flag, are part of it, just as were those regarding the Canadian flag with regard to the Union Jack. The recent ruling on the exclusion of the Canadian flag from the Quebec legislative assembly, except when the Queen's representatives are present, is another symbol of this phenomenon. Just as Canada did adopt its own national anthem,I believe that Quebec will also do so, as a signpost yet to come on the road travelled earlier by Canada.

The language legislation (i.e. Bill 101), and the use of language to assert the nature of Quebec society as francophone through its sign language law (Bill 178), are also relevant. The Allaire report, in its very title, *A Quebec Free to Choose*, is evidence of the thesis that I have proposed. Its recommendation of sweeping constitutional changes with increased or exclusive powers for Quebec in 22 jurisdictions is merely a step along the route I have been outlining and should not have come as a surprise. Nor, if I am right, would this be the end of the process.

Equilibrium and Chaos

What does my thesis imply for the final outcome? Would Quebec separate from Canada? A few concepts from economic theory seem to be very useful at this point: equilibrium, the dynamic path toward it, and chaos. Let me begin with the concept of equilibrium. I have adduced the strong primal gut feeling of *us* and *them* as the fundamental determinant of the process Quebec and Canada are going through. Economic considerations, laws and precedents, history and other ties are peripheral to this force. Given these assumptions, we can predict the theoretical equilibrium to be one of Quebec sovereignty *vis-à-vis* Canada, as we might have done *a priori* for Canada *vis-à-vis* Britain in the early years of this century.

Economic theory hammers into economists the realization that the actual dynamic path to an equilibrium is likely to be unpredictable. It must have been clear in the early 1920s that the theoretical equilibrium for Canada required its constitution to be patriated to Canada and the residual powers of the Westminster parliament to be eliminated. That did happen, but it took six decades of frustrating wrangling. The federal and provincial governments failed to reach an agreement under Mackenzie King in 1927, under Bennett in 1931, under St. Laurent in 1950, under Diefenbaker in 1960, under Pearson in 1964 and under Trudeau in 1971 before the actual patriation under Trudeau in 1982. Why did the successive prime ministers have to hammer at it, knowing that so many others had failed? I believe that my thesis provides an answer: Canada was a "distinct society" from Britain, we were *us*, Britain was *them* and we had to become masters in our own house. While this implied the final equilibrium of patriation of the Canadian constitution, as I have shown, the dynamic path and the time to equilibrium could not have been predictable.

This uncertainty must also be a characteristic of Quebec's path to its theoretical equilibrium of eventual sovereignty. The patriation of the Canadian constitution and the Canadian and Quebec Charters were part of this process, but by no means the beginning. The Meech Lake agreement was a further part of this process; a failed part, as were the various failed constitutional conferences on the patriation of the constitution. The Allaire report came next, as did the attempt to influence the dynamic path in the Bélanger-Campeau Commission report. But the pattern is essentially indeterminate.

Now we come to the concept of chaos. The path to patriation of the Canadian constitution was chaotic, its actual patriation was chaotic, its clauses were chaotic and its consequences have proven to be chaotic. Chaos is fundamental to the process of separation. Now, chaos theory does not deny the possibility of reaching equilibrium; it in fact assumes its existence and analyzes its properties, arguing that the particular values associated with that equilibrium are very sensitive to seemingly minor occurrences.

The sensitivity of equilibrium in a chaotic context such as the issue of Quebec's separation means that the particular aspects or clauses of the separation cannot be defined at this juncture. The eventual answer to how Canada's current public debt would be divided, and how the assets and liabilities of the Bank of Canada and of other Federal institutions would be partitioned, and other issues of that nature, belong to the chaotic equilibrium and cannot be known at this time. They will be eventually worked out, I suspect, in what is called the Canadian way: committees, compromises and tradeoffs, though after the fact of separation has been recognized.

I began by referring to the experience of first-generation Canadians and what that could tell us about the constitutional and sovereignty debates. What else can they really tell us? For one thing, small minorities don't count much in the outcome. Their concerns may be dragged as hurdles across the stage, and are often part of transitional provisions. But the very drive that produces the desire to be master in one's own house and the character of the nationalism that it engenders imply that the majority will (in any long-term sense) only determine the rights and the place of the minorities in its midst after the act of separation. This is not to imply that first-generation Quebeckers will be any worse off than first-generation Canadians in the Rest of Canada (ROC). It is just that they will live in a different milieu and be governed by different laws, as the other residents of these two countries (Quebec and ROC) will be also.

Economic Considerations

What about some of the other questions being debated? Is an independent Quebec feasible? It is hard to know what feasible means in this context. Does it mean slightly poorer (on the order of 5 per cent to 10 per cent lower per capita incomes than a Quebec in Canada) or very much poorer? If it is the former, with a possible decrease in incomes on the order of five per cent or so, it is irrelevant to the final decision on separation. Would any of us be willing to sacrifice our ideals and aspirations for such trifling differences? I believe not, nor do I think any countries would choose to forgo their autonomy or independence for such differences. And there is little possibility of large catastrophic declines in incomes.

In any case, I think that the economic experience of other countries which separated during the decolonization process gives us cause for optimism. Most did better after independence than they would have done otherwise, because they became free to determine which industries to promote, which to protect and which to open up to free international trade. Overall the economies grew and developed structures suited to each nation's resources and the abilities and the aptitudes of their people. But the point to note is that this wasn't necessarily, nor often, the pre-independence economic structure which had evolved in response to a different and larger overall economic unit. In the process of moving from the older structure appropriate to the pre-separation unit to the structure appropriate to the post-separation unit, certain industries declined and some were phased out, but others grew. Quebec industry, which relies upon the larger protected Canadian market, might well decline in the process. Milk production and textiles are possible examples, and employment in them may fall drastically. But there is no reason to assume that other industries will not take their place.

The point that I want to make, and which is often ignored in debates on the nuts and bolts of economics is that the determining factors for the prosperity of an independent Quebec are not the viability of its current industries but the underlying determinants of economic performance. And these underlying determinants of economic performance are the abilities of the people to take risks, to manage, to innovate, to learn, etc. There is no reason to assume that these are any worse in Quebec than in the ROC.

What about the issue of free trade or a customs union between an independent Quebec and a post-independence (and truncated) Canada? I would tend to focus here on the post-recrimination stage, for this stage is going to be transitory anyway and I choose to place my emphasis on the self-interest of nations. That self-interest, as exercised in the recent past on this continent, created a measure of free trade between the United States and Canada, and might create one between the United States, Canada and Mexico. If this is what current technology and the international context imply to be in the self-interest of the nations on this continent, then there is no reason to assume that this self-interest will cease to apply after the separation of Quebec.

Conclusion

I started by drawing upon the experience of first-generation Canadians in order to comment on the constitutional and sovereignty debates. My topic was not what these Canadians want the future of Canada to be, but it is worth saying a few words about it. They would prefer that Canada remain united. Further, the existence of two dominant cultures in Canada allows for greater tolerance of other cultures, while a separation creating unicultural states may diminish tolerance for immigrants. If Quebec did separate, it would want free trade and a free flow of peoples across the borders.

I see a great deal of similarity between the march of Canada toward separation from Britain and that of Quebec from Canada. In each case, to outsiders the cultures are virtually the same and the peoples not really different. Yet to the peoples themselves in the earlier case, there seemed to be vital differences; as time passed, one group felt that it could manage on its own and came to chafe "under" the other. With the patriation of the constitution, the flag and the national anthem, Canada is close to the end of that process of separation from Britain—close, but not at the end, for the Queen of England (who does not reside in Canada and whose outlook must be determined by Britain and its peoples, so different from those of Canada) is still Canada's monarch.

Quebec has now been moving along the same route for several decades. The patriation of the Canadian constitution in 1982 has provided a catalyst for this process. Bills 101 and 178, Meech Lake, and the Allaire and Bélanger-Campeau reports are landmarks along that route, as are the changes in symbols or the disputes about them. It seems that this process of separation may proceed to the same ultimate effect as the process of the separation of Canada from Britain, and may end in the sovereignty of Quebec *vis-à-vis* Canada.

But just as Canada and Britain are still bound by a common heritage and a shared history and culture, and are the best of friends, so too we should expect Quebec and the redefined Canada—with their shared history, heritage and cultures—to be close to each other and to be the best of friends. This need not mean being the closest trading partners, nor using a common language, nor using a common currency, nor using common laws. Friendship does not depend upon these; it is a matter of feelings. And out of these there are likely to emerge new and close links between the two countries that emerge out of Canada.

I have argued that the equilibrium state (given the present fundamental feelings of *us* and *them* in Quebec) is one of eventual separation with amicable relations in the post-separation state. Let me modify this prediction so as to provide you with some possibilities of non-separation. Theoretical predictions are always subject to the possibility of "random error," which could result in the eventual state stopping short of separation (or, alternatively, bias the result towards separation and hostility between the two emerging states). There is very considerable scope for such random errors since they would depend, among other things, on the personalities and ambitions of the major players as we move through the process. Let us hope that Quebec and Canada prove to be the exception, not the rule, and that they will stop short of separation.

Section V

Making Federalism Work

In Praise of the Status Quo

William G. Watson

THERE IS A TENDENCY THESE days to see the current constitutional crisis as marking a failure of Canadian federalism. I think this is wrong. It may ultimately mark the end of Canadian federalism. But federalism will not end because it has failed, but because Quebeckers have decided they want what federalism can never give them—nationhood. It might be argued that the mere fact of their wanting nationhood is evidence that federalism has failed. On the contrary; Canadian federalism helped produce a successful, modern society in Quebec, and this very success is the wellspring of Quebec's sovereignty movement. That children leave home is not always a sign of parental failure.

Measuring Federalism's Success

To my mind, there are two appropriate measures of a constitution's worth. One is the economic well-being of the citizens who live under it. The other is the degree of personal freedom they enjoy. By both these measures, the Canadian Constitution has been immensely successful. In terms of personal incomes we rank second in the world, and although personal freedom is much more difficult to measure we also rank high in the world tables in that. In addition, despite our interminable disputes, there is at street level considerable harmony among us, both as ethnic groups and as individuals. Even at Oka, the scene of our worst recent outbreak of civil strife, only one person was killed and he was not a native. It is yet another measure of our success as a society that we don't like to use "number of people killed per year in civil strife" as a measure, but it is the usual international standard and we do very well according to it.

No doubt we might have done better on all these counts under different constitutional arrangements. Perhaps with a different organizing document we would have had the world's highest living standard and its greatest personal freedom. That, unfortunately, is impossible to know. It may be heretical to say so but neither social scientists nor anyone else can know how Canada would have developed under a greatly different constitutional regime. Even informed guesses—and they would only be guesses—might be hopelessly wrong. Our predictive power in these matters is slight, though you would not know it to listen to most participants in the current debate about what will happen should Quebec secede.

Why the Breakup?

But if Canadian federalism is not a failure—quite the contrary—how is it that we are on the verge of a breakup?

To a certain extent, I agree with William Johnson's version of the causality. In a contemporary *trahison des clercs* [betrayal by intellectuals], Quebec intellectuals have conducted a vigorous and determined scapegoating in which federalism is at fault for most of what ails Quebec, and Pierre Elliott Trudeau—that horn-toed, slither-tailed, fork-tongued traitor to his people and their great national cause—is at fault for most of what ails federalism. I do not agree with Johnson that this is an uncommon syndrome, however. Most post-modern democratic societies seem very tolerant of scapegoating, so long as it is a majority that is being scapegoated. There are very few days these days when, as a white male teetering on the brink of middle age, I don't read something that blames me and people like me for somebody or other's problems. But the causality goes beyond that. It seems to me a country's sense of nationhood is always likely to be tenuous when it contains a large ethnic minority that is concentrated geographically and remains unassimilated. We live in a world of nation-states, and as a simple matter of logic many members of an ethnic minority are likely to think they, too, should be a country. This problem occurs in Spain, Belgium, Yugoslavia, Czechoslovakia, the Soviet Union, India, and any number of other countries, particularly federal countries, around the world.[1] It is not surprising that it should also occur in Canada. Pure reason aside, minorities have a strong self-interest in turning themselves into majorities. Countries that consist of ethnic communities are therefore almost bound to experience ethnic conflicts. If anything, the United States is the exception that proves the rule, though its recent history has hardly been characterized by ethnic calm.

The tensions to which ethnically diverse countries are prone have to be handled very carefully, though this is easier said than done. We Canadians should not get too down on ourselves simply because tensions have flared up again. We may not have had such a strong separatist movement before, but we have had periods in which relations between French and English, not to mention aboriginal and immigrant, have been extremely bitter. Whatever happens over the next few years, whether Quebec stays or goes, we are bound to have such tensions again.

A second generic difficulty is that, living so close to the United States,[2] virtually all Canadians, whatever their heritage, feel like an endangered species. We are also painfully aware that in terms of fame, power, influence—all the things that shouldn't count but do—the United States is a much more successful society than we are. As a result, many of us suffer from insecurity, even a sense of inferiority. This sense of inferiority is salted with a sense of injustice—because the things that shouldn't count do—and also, perversely, of superiority, since we feel we do have the better society, even if no one else in the world knows it. Finally, we are also a little angry at ourselves for envying the Americans their success at things we know we should disdain. The resulting, rather complicated psychological condition, which too many Canadians have analysed for too long, contributes to extreme sensitivity to slights, whether real or imagined. Try to get 26 million prickly people to make concessions to each other and you end up with things like the Meech Lake episode.

An Unbroken Chain of Historical Accidents

Given this perfectly normal Canadian environment of jealousy, tension and sensitivity, it does not take much to end the short periods of calm that over the years have interrupted our continuing constitutional turmoil. I would argue that what has got us into our latest fix is mainly an unfortunate series of mistakes and miscalculations—a chain of historical accidents—stretching back almost two decades now. To begin with, in the early 1970s, after three terms in office, Robert Bourassa's Liberal Party was perceived, probably correctly, as providing bad government. Unfortunately, the only credible opposition party was a separatist party. By voting out the Liberals,

Quebec thus committed itself to holding a referendum on separation even though a large majority of the population had absolutely no interest in it, as evidenced by the fact that a very soft referendum option proposed by a very popular premier was defeated 60-40.

The federal government of the day then adopted what in retrospect seems the unwise course of thorough constitutional reform while the separatist party was still in power in Quebec. Unfortunately, this federal government was itself in power only because of the Parliamentary muddle of December 1979, and its politically born-again leader knew this was the last chance to fulfill his lifelong ambition of a patriated constitution with an entrenched bill of rights. Of course, the reasonable presumption at the time was that the separatist party soon would be out of power, to be replaced by the official leader of the *Non* forces. But, in another historical accident, this leader proved so unappealing a figure that in fact the separatists remained in power, where they were bound to oppose any federal initiative that could plausibly be sold as answering Quebec's desire for renewed federalism.[3]

Nevertheless, the federal government went ahead with its reforms, which meant that Quebec was bound not to sign the agreement that eventually was arrived at. The bad taste this left in Quebeckers' mouths has been exaggerated in recent years, but a bad taste there undoubtedly was. Quebec having been isolated in this way, a combination of goodwill, self-interest, and naivety led a new federal government based partly in Quebec to initiate a Quebec Round of constitutional reform. Unfortunately, the only consensus agreed to by the premiers imposed the impossibly high test of unanimity. No doubt the Meech Lake Accord was imperfect; on the other hand, the Sermon on the Mount probably would not have got through the amending formula Meech faced.

Reasonable people should be able to agree that two major mistakes were made over the last decade. First, it was a mistake to undertake patriation with the separatists still in power in Quebec. Second, that mistake having been made, it was probably a mistake to try to repair it. But those who were willing to take the first risk in 1981-82 should not be so critical of the risk taken in 1987-89. Mackenzie King, one of the least regarded but most successful of Canadian prime ministers, clearly understood that in an ethnically divided society it does not pay to take large risks. If contemporary historians had not been so contemptuous of King's ofttimes calculated pusillanimity, contemporary prime ministers might have understood this better. But the fact is these errors were made. So it is surprising neither that we are where we are today, nor that most Canadians' sensitivities have been inflamed in the process of getting here.

The Lack of Substantive Grievances

Despite the cloud of ill-humour that currently hangs over our half of the continent, it is important to keep in mind that most people's constitutional grievances are almost entirely symbolic. To be precise: in my view Quebec has no serious substantive grievances with the current constitutional regime. The best way to demonstrate this is to ask what laws or policies we would have after separation that we could not have now. Those who propose separation almost never provide such a list. Quite the contrary; elaborate reassurances are given that most things would not change. In the area of language, for instance, does anyone seriously suggest that Quebec is unable to legislate sufficiently to secure the French language and culture?[4] Current arrangements allow it to outlaw English-only commercial signs even without resort to the notwithstanding clause, and to outlaw bilingual signs with it. (This under Trudeau's constitution.)

No doubt independence would permit the francophone majority to restrict minority language rights further, but most *indépendentistes* say they do not want this. As for economic policy, the powers an independent Quebec would need to conduct an even more interventionist industrial policy than it already has likely would be denied it by the terms of any free trade agreement it might wrest from the sharp dealers who run the U.S. Congress. Moreover, by continuing to use the Canadian dollar, which Jacques Parizeau says is what would happen, Quebec would give up any say in monetary policy. There is a good economic argument that jurisdictions of six million people shouldn't have their own monetary policies; unfortunately, most people have the contrary impression, that an independent monetary policy is a vital accoutrement of an independent country.

The fact that so little is supposed to change after separation suggests strongly that separation is an end in itself, and that the principal shortcoming of the status quo is not anything *in* it, but simply the fact that it is not separation. At bottom, I strongly suspect the fuss is mainly about flags, anthems and the design of government letterhead, though this obviously does not mean it is not serious.

I should immediately make clear that I take the same dim view of "western alienation." Over the last seven years most of the West's legitimate substantive grievances have been addressed. The West is outraged by the National Energy Policy? The National Energy Policy is removed. The West opposes the tariff? We get a Free Trade Agreement with the United States. The West feels underrepresented in Ottawa? Two of the three most powerful men in the government (Mazankowski and Clark), as well as the Governor General, are from the West. Western farmers are annoyed that Pierre Trudeau didn't sell their wheat? The government provides more than $1 billion a year to offset low grain prices. The West favours fiscal responsibility? The government limits increases in program spending to an average of three per cent (real) over its seven years in office.

True, some Westerners continue to be irked by official bilingualism. But in reality this policy imposes very few everyday obligations on them. It is true that unilingual Westerners, like unilingual Québecois, cannot become prime minister. But that is not a major constraint on most people, and it is worth remembering that one Westerner, Joe Clark, actually did become prime minister in recent years. At bottom, what Westerners don't like about Confederation—and I suspect this is what bothers most other complaining Canadians—is that their views don't dominate. Tough! Do a population count and you quickly see that Westerners' views shouldn't dominate. If they don't like being in a country where they are a minority, they should get out.

The same is true for Quebec. By any objective measure, Quebec has a very good deal in Confederation. In fact, that seriously understates matters, since Quebec has essentially run the federal government for the last thirty years. The even better deal it wants is to be both a country and a province at the same time. Fortunately, non-Quebeckers are in no mood to allow this. "Fortunately," because there would be grave dangers to that very successful society, English Canada, in the dramatic decentralization that would be required to effect it.

Scientific Federalism

Although it probably cannot succeed, an unholy alliance of Quebec, the western premiers, and the current federal government does seem likely to attempt such a decentralization. The strategy presumably will be to cloak Quebec's very special problems in the mantle of generalized regional alienation, and proceed with a large-scale devolution of powers. This will be done under the guise of what might be termed "scientific federalism," or "federalism for the twenty-first century," meaning federalism that will be efficient and will help us out-compete the Japanese. Whatever the name for it, it will be bogus, for the real agenda is to allow Quebec to scramble back in from the limb it clambered onto during its post-Meech spasm of nationalism.

There are several obvious proofs that scientific federalism is bogus. No one doubts there is duplication in our federalism. In theory, there are three ways of eliminating costly duplication. One is to give more powers exclusively to the federal government; the second, to give more powers to the provinces; and the third, to let people on their own do more things without regulation by government. But scientific federalism allows for only one of these options: decentralization to the provinces. If it were truly scientific, it would probably give the federal government exclusive control over areas such as the environment or corporate taxation, since lots of theory suggests that is where control should be. But it won't because that would require Quebec to surrender sovereignty, which Quebec will never do.

A second piece of evidence that scientific federalism is bogus is simply that if the Meech Lake Accord had passed no one would give a hoot about the efficiencies to be gained from reassigning powers.

Third, if our goal really is to compete with the Japanese, calling in the constitutional lawyers isn't the first thing most people would think of doing. News of our shiny new cost-efficient 21st-century constitution probably would not have them trembling in Tokyo.

Fourth, federalism is not a major reason for the economic problems we have (and we have fewer than is commonly believed). Most unitary states have trouble keeping up with the Japanese, too.

Fifth, it's not obvious that a constitution featuring a system of water-tight jurisdictional compartments is best. While it undoubtedly avoids duplication, it also prevents competition, and it is not at all clear that the gain from reduced duplication exceeds the loss from forgone competition. Local monopolies can do powerful damage.

A Federalist Lifebelt

Whatever the exact form of the deal, Quebec's federalists are now in such deep water (to change the metaphor) that federalists elsewhere in the country will have to throw them a lifebelt. The rhetoric is not hard to imagine. The separatist forces have peaked, it will be argued, but Quebec now needs a sign of goodwill, a sign that Canada is saying yes to Quebec. Unfortunately, the expression of goodwill will involve substantive changes in a constitution that, as I have argued, has been very successful. Because Quebec's separation from Canada would be very costly for both parties I believe such a deal should be struck, but only if the substantive changes in the constitution are minimal. For appearance's sake, it will not be possible to say that the exercise is mostly one of face-saving, but no one should be under any illusions that this is not what is going on. That is why I favoured the Meech Lake Accord, though the concessions that will be necessary this time around will go farther than Meech.

What Form Might a Lifebelt Take?

A minimal-change lifebelt presumably will include some sort of Senate reform, since after the disgrace of its G.S.T. "debate" the Senate no longer has any legitimacy—which is too bad since it finally has a sensible majority. It will also address the concerns of natives, although in addition to defining some sort of sovereignty for them it should also specify the obligations of their citizenship. It also will probably devolve one or two federal or shared powers—preferably the more frustrating ones, such as manpower planning—to the provinces. Which level gets these is not particularly important since no government is likely to do them well.

But the package should not go further than that. If it is not enough for Quebec, Quebec should be permitted to proceed to independence and Canada eventually should have an association with it. This is a drastic step, I realize, but if substantial devolution is the alternative, I prefer separation. If we're going to have a country, and not merely a geographic expression, it has to mean something when our representatives gather in Ottawa—even if, as I would greatly prefer, they generally decide not to engage in interventionist policies.

In this I differ fundamentally with Tom Courchene. In my view it is the act of deciding things together that constitutes nationhood, not the specifics of what we decide. Unlike Courchene, I believe it is possible to be a Canadian nationalist without being a social democrat. He would argue that equalization and programmes like it are the glue that keeps the country together. That seems to me to get things the wrong way round. Equalization and programs like it are expressions of our fellow-feeling; they do not cause it. Because we do have fellow-feeling for fellow citizens, we are not willing to tolerate their poverty. But these programs are a cost of nationhood, an obligation nationhood imposes on us. If anything, once in place they are corrosive of nationhood, an acid and not a glue. At the first sign of ungratefulness on the part of the recipients, we resent having to support them. Because they are family, we help the poor cousins. But the help doesn't reinforce "family-ness", it strains it; the poor cousins are resentful that they must have help, and we donors resent their resentfulness.

A Few Kind Words for Middle-aged White Males

I will close with brief remarks about the process by which these constitutional amendments should take place, but I want to preface that with a few kind words for white middle-aged men meeting in closed rooms. This subspecies is widely blamed for the Meech Lake fiasco and there is almost universal agreement—even the subspecies apparently agrees!—that it will not be permitted to dominate the next round of constitutional change.

First, some middle-aged white men are quite smart and many have much experience in constitutional matters. Experience is not always a hindrance to good decision making, so their contribution to the process can be valuable. Second, most of the country being white—only six per cent is "visible minority"—it is neither surprising, unnatural, nor undesirable that most decision makers are white. Third, most of the country is middle-aged, at least using the old definition that no one over thirty can be trusted. Of course, the many fashionable foulups caused by the trendy youth movements of the 1960s and 1970s should have taught us that, as far as governing is concerned, only people over thirty can be trusted.

Fourth, while it is true that most of the country is not male, if the non-male majority does not like being governed by males, it shouldn't vote for them. Non-males and non-whites together have a majority of the vote. Fifth, regarding the complaint that decisions are made behind closed doors, anyone who has attended a university senate meeting knows that meaningful negotiation, even about the most trivial matters, can seldom be done in public. Sixth, I concede there is a good argument for having the public ratify whatever constitutional agreement is struck. Giving the public responsibility might in fact make it more responsible. On the other hand, the public is in many ways a beast. If we had direct democracy in Canada, we would also have capital punishment, highly restricted immigration, and no Free Trade deal. We might not even belong to GATT. Though I might let the public ratify the rules under which we all are to live, I'm sure I don't want it writing them.

Finally, despite popular contempt for our parliamentary institutions, they have overwhelming legitimacy going all the way back to 1215. This would not be true of any institution invented in 1991 or 1992.

Against a Constituent Assembly

I am therefore opposed to any notion that our problems should be handed over to a group of inspired amateurs, as the proponents of a constituent assembly would have us do. Even if such an assembly were practicable, the *status quo* is not nearly so horrific as to justify such a radical departure from our normal ways of doing business. Questions of principle aside, I can't believe an assembly would be practicable. How would it be chosen? What powers would it have? And who would decide how it would be chosen and what powers it would have? If we can't solve well-worked problems such as Senate reform, how in the world are we to make radical and complicated decisions about a constituent assembly, and in short order? And who will be making such decisions? Presumably the same discredited white middle-aged males who are held responsible for our problems in the first place. If we don't trust them to run the current system, how can we trust them to invent a new one?

If Quebec's Bélanger-Campeau Commission is the model for the desired process, it is a bad model. The "public" members of Bélanger-Campeau were in fact leaders of various interest groups. The last thing Canada needs is to have its constitution rewritten by people who are compelled by particular interests. It would be much better, as William F. Buckley has often suggested, to draw one hundred people randomly from the country's telephone books.

Finally, there seems to be an implicit assumption among the proponents of a constituent assembly that our politicians have been unable to arrive at a constitutional accommodation mainly because they are politicians, and that if only a group of amateurs sat down to study the problem they would come to agreement quite expeditiously. In fact, by now it probably has gotten through to politicians that their apparently interminable bickering has seriously annoyed the public. They presumably would like nothing more than to come to a final constitutional settlement. The trouble is, there are deep disagreements in the country about what should be done. These disagreements will not be resolved simply because the decision making is handed over to a different group of people. If the group is representative of the population, it is bound to disagree; if it is not, it will not have legitimacy.

Minimal Change—or Separation

We should not underestimate the divisions that currently exist in the country. One province won't allow the national flag to be flown in its legislature. It is hard to imagine this occurring in any other federal country—any other federal country not on the verge of a break-up, that is. The same province will not allow one of the country's two official languages to appear on commercial signs. Of course, the other official language is booed when the national anthem is sung in it at sporting events in Toronto, even though this is frequently the only time many of the boo-ers—they are also boors—hear French spoken.[5]

By any reasonable standard, these are trivial provocations. On the other hand, they are symptomatic of strong disaffection on both sides of the linguistic divide. We must face the possibility plainly that the disaffections may now be irreparable, that we may in fact end up going our separate ways. I sincerely hope not, because that would be extremely costly, not least to English Quebeckers, of whom I am one. But there are some things that would be more costly than a breakup. The end of English Canada would be one. It is therefore crucial that we not adopt the attitude that we must do anything and everything, including the drastic decentralization that would threaten the survival of English Canada, to keep Quebec in.

If Quebec and Canada did break up, we would still be neighbours. More importantly, many aspects of our national life would not change. The snow would continue to fall; the Northern Lights would continue to shine; hockey would continue to be played; the sap would still flow in the maple trees (assuming the proposed maple marketing board didn't have them all chopped down); the Americans still would know very little about us; people would have to earn a living; trade would take place. No doubt the world would be a slightly worse place. It probably would not end.

Notes

[1] "Too many 'nations', too few states," writes Walter Russel Mead in a review of the "New Europe" in April 1991's *Harper's*. "...[A]ll the people who hate each other too much to live in the same country. It's not just the Soviets and Yugoslavs who talk about breaking the ties that bind them. Thirty miles from Vienna, there are Slovaks who can't bear to live under the same flag as the Czechs. It's much the same thing—though not the same crisis just now—to the west: the Irish nationalists in the British Isles; the Basques in Spain...Welcome to the oldest of Europes, seething dangerously beneath the New..." (p. 47).

[2] "So close to the United States and so far from God," as the Mexicans say. One benefit of closer relations with Mexico has been learning that there are other people who share our neuroses concerning the Americans.

[3] One thing I am tired of hearing is that in 1980 Quebeckers said yes to Canada. In voting for "renewed federalism," which now seems to be the officially accepted inference concerning what happened, Quebeckers said a loud maybe to Canada. Or, more precisely, to themselves: the referendum was Quebec's idea, not the rest of the country's. It was answering its own question, not Canada's. Canada saying no to Quebec during the Meech round—which, of course, is not what it did say—would therefore have been entirely understandable.

[4] The whole notion is a conceit, of course. Short of Stalinist measures, legislation cannot protect languages and cultures, but in our own case that is equally true under the current constitution as under Quebec independence.

[5] This is such a regular occurrence now that in some cases the authorities no longer insist on having the bilingual version of the anthem sung.

The American Indian on the Reservation: Powerful or Powerless?

Verna Lawrence

An American Apartheid

I AM OF INDIAN DESCENT, an elected city official, and for some years I have been involved in various aspects of the "Indian issue" throughout the United States. When I became involved, I was shocked to discover the media silence which prevailed. It was nearly impossible to get any information on Indian problems. We had to dig for facts and often ran into a brick wall. To say that the news media was reluctant to print anything reflecting on the Indian is an understatement.

Unfortunately it is still true to a great extent that the Indian issue with all its various and associated problems is not being discussed publicly. These problems will never be solved until they are examined objectively, honestly, and with an open mind, free of any accusation of racial bias and free from the great American guilt syndrome.

The American Indian on the reservation is in a unique situation. Indians were forced onto reservations by the U.S. government so they could be controlled. Many Indians resisted to the death the segregation and isolation of their people. Unfortunately, the control still exists today in this American form of apartheid. Generally speaking, the Indian person on the reservation owns no land, has no equity and has no collateral. He is powerless and is kept powerless. He does not have the same rights as you and I, as the tribal constitution takes precedence on the reservation. The definition of sovereign is "supreme in power or authority; to have supreme authority; to possess power to govern without external control; to exercise supreme political power in a state." This is what the U.S. reservations have in the United States. In Canada, the reserves do not have sovereignty, but in the United States we have tribal sovereignty.

A fundamental feature of the U.S. constitutional system is the division of political authority between two levels of government—state and national. The states under the federal system are units in the formation of a nation, not governments independent of a nation, and the powers of the national government are such as are granted to it by the Constitution of the United States. There are no others. The basic principle was implied but not expressed in the Constitution as first adopted. So important was its expression in the constitutional regard that the Tenth Amendment provides that powers not delegated to the United States are reserved to states respectively or to the people. The states gave up certain powers in establishing the national government. They set out these powers in a written document and expressly reserved all other powers to themselves or to the people.

Tribal Sovereignty Implications

The tribal government tells us they are a supreme power, but *Durrel vs. Rena* (a Supreme Court decision of May 1990) points out that tribes are not only dependent sovereigns but are limited sovereigns, and that their authority extends only to their voluntary tribal membership and only to tribal land. Tribes and individuals owe their allegiance to the greater sovereign, the United States, as do the individual states. It is a strange irony that tribes do not actually own the land that all their benefits are linked to solely on the base of their race. The land is held in trust for them by the United States government, but is owned in the name of the federal government. Yet tribes can buy more land, put it in trust, create new reservations, extend their jurisdiction, their zoning, their codes, their ordinances, and their taxes, thus thwarting city, county, township or state jurisdictions.

In our community (Sault Ste. Marie, Michigan), where we have a reservation within our corporate limits, we have a tribe that has an economic development commission. Since on the reservation there are no taxes, the tribe can compete unfairly with the city, the county, the state, and entice businesses onto the reservation. But the privilege is a two-edged sword. Many businesses or companies that go onto the reservation end up being taxed by the tribe.

This leads to many problems for my community. Not only is it frustrating to deal with, it is excessively expensive, as we have to fight for our own tax dollars with the U.S. government. Many times the tribes will sue the city, the state, the county. We as an entity, city-tribe-state, cannot sue the tribe; they have sovereign immunity. We must sue the United States government in the name of the tribe, an expensive proposition. And this is using tax dollars to protect one's own area, again because of the sovereign immunity. I'm stressing the sovereign immunity—sovereignty—because in Canada the tribes do not have sovereignty. But this is what the tribes in Canada are asking for: tribal sovereignty. Beware!

The United States Department of the Interior has trusteeship over the Indians—their property, their way of life, and their future. The Department of the Interior is bound to represent Indian interests to approve or disapprove contracts, approve or disapprove ordinances, assess impacts and long-term value of our natural resources on Indian land, and exercise control of Indians, their land, and their natural resources. Congress has ultimate authority over Indian affairs, and tribes depend on Congress to continue or expand benefits over and above outdated treaty awards. Most of the treaties were made in the 19th century in our country, the same as in Canada. We near the year 2000. How long are we going to pay for those treaties? How many times are we going to pay for land? How many attorneys are we going to hire to protect people's property? In the state of Wisconsin, to give you an example of the abuse of a natural resource, the Supreme Court of Wisconsin has ruled that the tribes in northern Wisconsin can go on private property to hunt and fish in private lakes. This invites confrontation. This is when you have riots. This is what you in Canada must beware of. We've got problems in the United States. Yours are just starting to surface, but we've got plenty. In Wisconsin, a tribe is claiming 65,000 acres—of farmland, an airport, and part of a city—and land titles are all tied up. Until litigation ceases, you can't buy or sell property. This is why people feel so strongly about this issue. Land claim problems have begun to surface in Canada, and there is more to come. Beware.

Congress, as I noted earlier, has ultimate authority over Indian Affairs, and tribes depend on Congress to continue or expand benefits. These added benefits bestowed upon tribe or tribal leaders seldom filter down to the poor Indian. Do you know what a tribal chief makes? One I know makes $116,000 a year, plus expenses, and he doesn't live on the reservation. If government grants filtered down to the poor Indian, this would impede tribal control and destroy the image which is needed and used to get more and more funding. The tribal members are not able to object; they rely on tribal authorities for benefits and they feel the need for real or implied retaliation against government when grants are not forthcoming.

The people on the reservation do not have the same guaranteed rights that you and I do. On the reservation, the tribal constitution takes precedence over the U.S. Constitution and the Bill of Rights. They do not have the guarantees of our basic civil rights and have no recourse when their rights are violated. Think of it—no freedom of speech, no guarantee of a free trial due to the extent of nepotism in tribal courts, plus no qualifications needed to be a judge. There is no Freedom of Information Act, and there is no Open Meetings Act. Reservation residents are not able to get information on tribal actions or expenditures, so tribes are not accountable either to their members or to those who support them, the American taxpayers. Yet tribes are making repeated demands and claiming more resources, even saying that they never ceded the Great Lakes to the United States. Appeasement of tribal demands does not work and agreements with tribes are not binding. When new leadership comes in, prior agreements are ignored. Archaic treaties with the tribes are the vehicles used to hold our scarce and dwindling natural resources hostage—water, minerals, coal, wildlife, fish. All our natural resources including those on 53 million acres of Indian trust land must be used properly, protected from misuse and exploitation, in order to be of benefit to all our citizens for future generations. In the past, the courts have handed down ultraliberal interpretations of treaties, not considering the intent of the treaties at the time they were made or their impact on resources.

There are numerous examples of present-day Indian claims, but I'm just going to go over some information I have from the Great Lakes. A recent Indian newspaper informs us that American and Canadian tribes are going to have a water rights claim on the Great Lakes. That will be disastrous for both countries. I am on a bi-national committee for the cleaning up of the lake between Sault, Ontario and Sault, Michigan and it is considering a contract between the State of Michigan, the Province of Ontario, the U.S. government, and the federal government of Canada.

Some tribal people attended the meeting, and they wanted to be recognised as a *nation* in that agreement. The agreement we completed was between two nations, the U.S. and Canada; that's it. So this is what you have to be careful of. Once you give the tribes sovereignty, they can come in and ask and get to be recognised as a nation. I stress that this is what you must be careful of. We are correct in our concern regarding our natural resources throughout the whole of the U.S. and Canada. If the tribes are granted sovereignty, we must make all our citizens aware of the possible impact on life itself when one racial group gains the ability to turn off the tap and cannot even be sued since it has sovereign immunity.

There is an ongoing attempt to discourage critical examination of federal Indian policy and archaic Indian treaties by labelling critics as racists. This racist labelling is an attempt to protect tribes and treaties from close scrutiny, which would destroy any illusion that has been created to gloss over injustices and glorify a perceived but nonexistent ancient lifestyle that was lost when Indians embraced the dominant culture and the creature comforts that went along with it. The people on the reservation are not going to give up their water, their automobiles, or their refrigerators; they have accepted the dominant culture.

No amount of money can make amends for past mistakes, and in the case of the American Indian, those who were wronged are long dead along with those who committed the wrongs. Anyone who has traced their ancestry can find inequities which they could apply to themselves if they choose to wallow in self-pity. We must not be swayed or intimidated by feelings of guilt or taunts of racism, or the Indian issue will never be resolved.

A Proposal: Canadian Bilingual Districts by Democratic Choice

R.S. McCall

SUGGESTIONS HAVE RECENTLY BEEN MADE to the effect that the federal policy of official bilingualism over the last 20 years has been a failure, and that Ottawa should now abandon the policy and transfer all powers over language to the provinces. In our opinion, for Canada to move away from official bilingualism, and in doing so to betray a tradition which has been central to its existence since 1867, is unthinkable. At the same time, we recognize the legitimate objections of those who do not want another language forced upon them. We sympathize with those who fear that they will be numbered in the swelling ranks of the unemployed for lack of bilingual competence.

What follows is a constructive proposal which we believe will preserve the essential character of Canadian bilingualism, remain true to our bilingual tradition without forcing it on people who do not want it, and finally strengthen both Quebec and Quebec's ties with the rest of Canada. Is this an impossibility? No, it is not.

As a first principle, there can be no backtracking on federal coast-to-coast bilingual policies: bilingual labelling, the right to a criminal trial in French or English, minority language education rights as enshrined in the Charter, bilingual services in airports and railway stations, the right to correspond with and receive notices from the federal government in either official language, etc. We take this as a basic premise of life anywhere in Canada, and if it were abolished we could no longer recognize the resulting country as the land of our birth.

But above and beyond these coast-to-coast principles, further bilingualism should be free, not forced. By this we mean that the decision of a municipality or other territory to constitute itself a bilingual district should be a democratic one, and that all regions of Canada should be given the chance to become officially bilingual if they so choose. This is a radical proposal in these days of top-down decision making, but it is one that can succeed where others fail.

The proposal to base territorial bilingualism on democratic choice rather than, say, a certain minimum percentage of minority language speakers would permit districts to opt for it even where the number of minority language speakers was low. It would also cover provinces which do not currently provide for bilingual districts. New Brunswick is already officially bilingual. In Ontario, which recognizes bilingual districts on a demographic basis, the proposal would permit other districts to become bilingual if they so desired. In Quebec, and in provinces where there are minority francophone communities, our proposal would entitle areas to become officially bilingual if they so chose. And, of course, only if they so chose.

The advantage of such a system is that the people who decided to make their district bilingual would have a strong stake in making official bilingualism work. In this respect the proposal is similar to the creation of French immersion programs in schools, which has been extraordinarily successful in all parts of Canada. The existence of this network is a strong force binding Canada together. It owes its success to the fact that it came into being because people wanted it, not because they were told they had to have it.

This is the essence of our proposal. In Quebec and, we are certain, in other provinces too, there are people who want to live bilingually, who feel that their lives are enriched by a bilingual environment.

Our proposal is that in a community where a majority of the people wish it, and where this wish is expressed and recorded democratically, they should be permitted to create and/or declare their affiliation with a bilingual district. The boundaries of this district would be determined by the place of residence of those who want it.

What would be the powers of a bilingual district? What degree of official bilingualism would it incorporate? Certainly it would prohibit any kind of discrimination based on language. Beyond that, would it involve bilingual parking tickets? Access to bilingual health and social services? The power to communicate with the provincial government in either French or English? These questions would remain to be worked out. But the principle of democratic choice in working them out would have to be respected.

For Montreal, the creation of an officially bilingual district along the lines suggested would represent an extremely attractive option. Such a district, with guarantees for its bilingual character, would attract attention, people and corporations from around the world. It would be a powerful source of economic prosperity not only for the district but for the whole province. The economy of Montreal is at present in decline, and the creation of a guaranteed bilingual district would be a valuable stimulus.

Finally, bilingual districts both in Quebec and in the other provinces could serve as bonds which tie Canada together. In contrast to suggestions that Canada should resign itself to moving towards a unilingual Quebec and a unilingual Rest of Canada, bilingual districts remain true to the spirit of Confederation. Canadians who wish to preserve the unity and integrity of our country should support the idea, and work for the creation of an officially bilingual district in the area in which they live.

American Federalism:
Keeping Government Safe

A. R. Riggs and Tom Velk

IN ITS PLANNING STAGE THE title for this symposium was "Federalism in North America," but as a crisis over provincial powers deepened here we decided that Canada's dilemma commanded priority status. And so, as the symposium winds down, it may be appropriate to remind everybody that the United States, once also branded "the sick man of the continent," recovered from civil war and has since flourished for over a century under an unchanged constitution, give or take a few amendments. Article V of the document provides that whenever two-thirds of the state legislatures so desire a new constitutional convention may be called, but the device has never been used.

Popular Sovereignty

What makes the American version of federalism endure? Economic interests, political necessity, culture, geography and the people of the various states, from Maine to Hawaii and Alaska, are far from homogeneous. We believe that what renders legitimacy to law in the United States is a tradition of popular sovereignty together with a narrow range of permissible action by government. Individual liberty, defined in the Constitution itself and in the first ten amendments or Bill of Rights, permanently excludes certain state actions. Obedience to federal power is guaranteed by a fierce allegiance to popular sovereignty, and by a process from 1787 that historian Edmund Morgan called "the invention of an American people."[1] *Popular sovereignty*, as Morgan sees it, is a self-evident truth, or rather a "fiction" upon which the entire American experiment with republican government rests.[2]

This was not always so. For eight years, from 1781 to 1789, the United States stumbled along under a loose confederation where sovereignty clearly resided in the individual states. The Continental Congress, composed of delegates chosen by state legislatures and burdened with debt, could borrow money but could not impose taxes; it could pass resolutions but could make no laws; it could negotiate treaties but was unable to enforce them. And in what passed for a national assembly tiny obstructive Rhode Island had an equal say with mighty Virginia.

Something needed to be done, and it is widely believed that the so-called Founding Fathers at the Constitutional Convention of 1787 flagrantly increased the scope of national authority by usurping power from the states. If the collective powers of government had then been limited and finite, this might be a plausible explanation for what happened. The states did relinquish their sovereignty. But the irony of the convention lies in a figurative sleight-of-hand. Sovereignty, snatched from the states by James Madison's Constitution, was handed not to the federal government but to the people. The first three words of the preamble, "We the people," announced it, and a ratification process by elected conventions drove the point home. And in creating the House of Representatives, Madison (as Morgan writes) invented "a sovereign American people to overcome the sovereign states."[3]

The efforts of James Madison fell short of his goals. He did not at that time get popular election of senators and the President, or a veto by Congress over state legislation. But he entrenched in the Constitution concurrent and separated powers, checks and balances, and an independent judiciary which almost immediately began to review laws, state and federal, for their constitutionality. Powers not clearly defined in the document were reserved for the states or the people under the Tenth Amendment, but from the beginning the courts were far more vigorous in striking down state legislation than in challenging federal law, the supreme law of the land.

Other Safeguards Considered

Can the courts, checks and balances, the distribution of powers on many levels, and a Bill of Rights that will not tolerate exceptions, keep government safe? James Madison claimed that there was far less danger of corruption leading to abuse of power in the national arena than in that of the states. Seizing upon an insight from David Hume's "Idea of a Perfect Commonwealth," Madison argued in "Federalist 10" that the larger the voter constituency, the fewer opportunities existed for chicane. "Extend the sphere," he said, "and you take in a greater variety of parties and interests; you make it less probable that a majority of the whole will have a common motive to invade the rights of other citizens."[4]

Aside from corruption, what other dangers threatened Madison's plans for keeping government safe? In the 19th century, commentators including John C. Calhoun of South Carolina were obsessed with the possible or real threat of a tyranny of the majority. The subject got a thorough airing in the 1830's because Calhoun exploited Southern discontent and because Alexis de Tocqueville marked it as the gravest potential danger to the republic in his famous two-volume critique, *Democracy in America.*

Calhoun, spokesman for a southern minority that wished to retain its system of slavery, proposed what he called the rule of the concurrent or geographical majority, the idea being that an individual state, or a group of like-thinking states, should have the authority to nullify a federal law if it displeased them. Needless to say, this would have restored state sovereignty, potentially impaired the rights of individual citizens—minorities within states—and replaced American federalism with a superficially weak and impotent confederation. Citizens outside the South were hostile to, even outraged by, such a proposal.

Alexis de Tocqueville, back in France after viewing what he believed to be Europe's eventual fate, was also critical of the majority will, but his writings did not displease Americans. The absolute sovereignty of the people, universal suffrage, and democratic majorities, said de Tocqueville, are not enough to keep government safe. Protection of minorities through a free press and certain safeguards built into the Constitution, particularly a decentralization of power through vigorous state and local initiatives, and in the courts which interpret the Bill of Rights, are not enough. Americans lack vigilance in protecting their liberty; equality tends to make the citizens complacent and conservative—to let government do what it will. This, de Tocqueville feared, could eventually lead to a centralization of power, to a government which would be benignly despotic.[5]

De Tocqueville's critique (I have seen the future, and it may not work) quickly drew the attention of the young English philosopher John Stuart Mill, who reviewed the book in London. The author of *Democracy in America* then wrote Mill that he was the only one who understood the message. "I keep it [the review] carefully," the Frenchman wrote, "to prove to myself that it really is possible to understand me."[6] Mill did not get around to dealing with de Tocqueville's message until he composed his famous "Essay on Liberty" in 1859. In this work Mill repeated a startling number of assumptions that de Tocqueville voiced years before. Then Mill asked a question that the Frenchman did not consider: What are "the nature and limits of the power which can be legitimately exercised by society over the individual?"[7] Mill wished to establish some guidelines, some general rules.

Here Mill's devotion to the Utilitarian views of Jeremy Bentham made his answer almost predictable. Utilitarianism taught that government should promote the greatest good for the greatest number. But what if, in pursuing that estimable prospect, government stepped upon the legitimate rights of the minority? In pursuing the greatest good for the greatest number, does a government have the moral right to pass *any* law? Mill's answer was an emphatic no.[8] "The only part of the conduct of any one, for which he is amenable to society is that which concerns others" Mill wrote.[9] This is reinforced latter on: "As soon as any part of a person's conduct affects prejudicially the interests of others, society has jurisdiction over it."[10] But Mill hastened to add,

> The only purpose for which power may be rightfully exercised over any member of a civilized community, against his will, is to prevent harm to others. His own good, either physical or moral, is not a sufficient warrant.[11]

It is not clear whether Mill was writing with an eye on the American Constitution, but he keyed himself into an American controversy. And just as de Tocqueville had concentrated on analytical matters and ignored general guidelines for the application of power by government, Mill chose not to deal with how a minority ought to react to abuse of power by the majority. This was a question of great moment in the United States at the time as North and South drifted toward civil war. Thus Henry David Thoreau, resident of Concord, Massachusetts, had sought an alternative method to that of Calhoun by which his minority, a minority that opposed slavery and the Mexican War in the 1840's, might resist the majority will.

In 1849 Thoreau published his answer in the now famous essay, "Civil Disobedience."

Thoreau agreed, as Mill did, that a majority is often wrong.[12] How then should the minority to a law or an action express its displeasure? Thoreau answered that there is one effective response to immorality: defy the law and accept the consequences. "If [government] is such a nature that it requires you to be an agent of injustice to another," he said, "then I say break the law. Let your life be a counter-friction to stop the machine."[13] Petitions are of no avail in the face of a massive injustice. "Under a government which imprisons any unjustly," Thoreau said, "the true place for a just man is also a prison. A minority is powerless," he added, "while it conforms to the majority; it is not even a minority then; but it is irresistible when it clogs by its whole weight. If the alternative is to keep all just men in prison, or give up war and slavery, the State will not hesitate which to choose."[14]

It must be stressed, however, that none of the three commentators we have discussed from the 19th century favoured appeasement of minorities by reducing the legitimate functions of the state, or changing its structure to accommodate dissent. On the contrary, de Tocqueville was impressed with the vigour and vitality of government in the United States, and he cautioned that weaker confederations had never survived.[15] Mill also had no intention of de-energizing government, and Thoreau, after saying "That government is best which governs not at all" in his opening sentence, admitted later that he "merely wanted a better government."[16] All were concerned instead with the abuse of power, or the potential abuse of power, by unchecked majorities, and all believed in permanent decentralization of power. De Tocqueville, as a member of the Chamber of Deputies in the 1840s, advocated decentralization of government in France and an independent judiciary, which he had praised in the United States. And Thoreau, reacting to laws that he deemed violations of the Bill of Rights, advocated not rebellion, but constitutional litigation.

Conclusion

We asked earlier, What makes the American version of federalism endure? Our answer was that popular sovereignty, a self-evident fiction, and clearly defined limitations on what the state may legitimately do, are the keys to longevity. As Thomas Jefferson wrote to James Madison when the Constitution of the United States was up for ratification in 1787,

> I have a right to nothing, which another has a right to take away... Let me add, that a bill of rights is what the people are entitled to against any government on earth, general or particular, and what no just government should refuse, or rest on inference.[17]

De Tocqueville wrote that "it is in the nature of all governments to seek constantly to enlarge their sphere of action,"[18] and Jefferson left us with his warning that the price of freedom is eternal vigilance. We believe that so long as the debate continues, the encouraging prospect remains for keeping government safe.

Notes

[1] Edmund S. Morgan, *Inventing the People* (New York, N.Y., 1988).

[2] *Ibid.*, pp. 13-15.

[3] *Ibid.*, p. 267.

[4] Roy P. Fairfield, ed., *The Federalist Papers* (Garden City, N.Y., 1966), p. 22.

[5] Alexis de Tocqueville, *Democracy in America*; Phillips Bradley, ed. (New York, N.Y., 1945), I, p. 311.

[6] *Ibid.*, II, p. 411.

[7] John Stuart Mill, "On Liberty," in *The Utilitarians* (Garden City, N.Y., 1961), p. 475.

[8] *Ibid.*, p. 483.

[9] *Ibid.*, p. 484.

[10] *Ibid.*, p. 553.

[11] *Ibid.*, p. 484.

[12] Henry David Thoreau, "Civil Disobedience," in Loren Baritz, ed., *Sources of the American Mind* (New York, N.Y., 1966), p. 346.

[13] *Ibid.*, p. 351.

[14] *Ibid.*, p. 353.

[15] De Tocqueville, I, pp. 162-63.

[16] Thoreau, pp. 345-46.

[17] Adrienne Koch and William Peden, eds., *The Life and Selected Writings of Thomas Jefferson* (New York, N.Y., 1972), p. 438.

[18] De Tocqueville, I, p. 311.

Printed in Canada